D1579946

Telephone: 0207 487 7449
E-mail: Library @ regents.ac.uk

This book is due for return on or before the latest date listed below

Shakespeare

Jacobean Shakespeare

Peter Milward, S.J.

EX CORDE
ECCLESIAE

VERITATIS SPLENDOR

·AVE·
MARIA
UNIVERSITY

Sapientia Press
of Ave Maria University

Cover Images:

James I, half-length portrait by Critz, John de, the Elder (ca. 1552–1642). © Roy Miles Fine Paintings/The Bridgeman Art Library.

G.11631.B.L. Title Page with a Portrait of Shakespeare, from Mr William Shakespeare's Comedies, Histories and Tragedies, edite. © British Library, London, UK/© British Library Board. All Rights Reserved/The Bridgeman Art Library.

Cover Design: Eloise Anagnost

Printed in the United States of America.

Library of Congress Control Number: 2006928347

ISBN-10: 1-932589-33-3

ISBN-13: 978-1-932589-33-7

Table of Contents

chapter 1
Jacobean Heroines

W<small>HAT A CONTRAST</small> is here between the general title *Jacobean Shakespeare* and the contents, which are seemingly concentrated on the heroines of Shakespeare's Jacobean plays! What, it may be asked, about such outstanding heroes as Othello and Lear, who have given their names to the tragedies in which they appear? And what, for a further example, about Prospero in the final romance of *The Tempest*? They are all, I agree, outstanding characters, each in his own drama, but on mature consideration I find that at least in his Jacobean plays—with one or two notable exceptions—Shakespeare has for reasons of his own (at which I try to guess) concentrated rather on the heroines than on the heroes. Even in the above-mentioned cases I dare to say that Desdemona is more important for him than Othello, and Cordelia more important for him than Lear. As for *The Tempest*, we have Prospero's own word for it in his opening conversation with Miranda that "I have done nothing but in care of thee" (i.2).

As for the other plays, Isabella is so much the heroine of *Measure for Measure* that she leaves us in some doubt whether to assign the hero's part to the duke-friar or to the unjust judge Angelo. Then, too, Helena is so much the heroine of *All's Well That Ends Well* as to leave her unworthy husband Bertram altogether in the shade. As for *Macbeth*, it is obviously Lady Macbeth, rather than her henpecked husband, who (as we say) "wears the trousers". Then in the doubly named *Antony and Cleopatra*, as in the previous *Romeo and Juliet*, it is Cleopatra who is the principal partner in their duo. Only in *Coriolanus*—by way of exception, as there have to be exceptions to every rule—does the somewhat colourless hero stand out above his three womenfolk, even his "dragon" of a mother, Volumnia. Even more of an exception is *Timon of Athens*, whose principal defect as a drama—and possibly the main reason why it was left unfinished—is its lack of a heroine. Only with Shakespeare's *vita nuova* in *Pericles* do we come upon a series of ideal heroines for whom each play seems to be specially designed—not only for Marina in that play, but also for Imogen in *Cymbeline*, for Perdita in *The Winter's Tale*, leading up to Miranda in *The Tempest*. To this series we may also add Katharine in the collaborative play of *Henry VIII*, of whom Dr. Johnson remarked that the genius of Shakespeare comes in and goes out with her.

It is also thanks in large measure to these Jacobean heroines, from Desdemona onwards, that we may notice a complete break in atmosphere and dramaturgy between the Elizabethan and the Jacobean Shakespeare. Towards the end of Elizabeth's forty-five-year reign our attention is drawn to that odd succession of trivial titles attached to such comedies as *Much Ado About Nothing*, *As You Like It*, and *Twelfth Night*, or *What You Will*. It all serves to leave us with the impression that the dramatist couldn't be bothered with the titles, or that, as with Hamlet, there must have been "something in his soul o'er which his melancholy sits on brood" (iii.1). Then, there are so many characters in the late Elizabethan plays, whether comedies or tragedies, such as Antonio and Portia, Rosalind, Cassius, and, above all, Hamlet, who can't hide their weariness but indulge in laments like that of the last-mentioned hero: "How weary, stale, flat, and unprofitable / Seem to me all the uses of this world!" The play of *Hamlet*, moreover, which is commonly paired with *Troilus and Cressida* as two late Elizabethan "problem tragedies", may be seen as offering a fitting farewell to the old Elizabethan age, as at once climax and anticlimax, leaving both the play and its hero with an uneasy feeling of unfulfilled promise.

Then, what a difference there is between such a world-weary play as *Hamlet* and Shakespeare's first Jacobean tragedy of *Othello*! And what a difference there is, we may add, between the poor Ophelia and the divine Desdemona! What, we may well wonder, is the cause of this difference, which appears as well in the plays as in their respective heroines? The obvious cause may be laid at the feet of the different monarchs, the old Tudor queen with all her frailty (as of Gertrude) and her failings (as of Cressida), on the one hand, and the new Stuart king with his promise of a new policy of religious toleration, on the other—though it was a promise destined to remain unfulfilled. For in those days, as not today, periods of English history were largely dominated by the personality of the monarch. And for Shakespeare's own company in particular, there was all the difference in the world between the old Chamberlain's Men—despite the legendary favour shown them by the queen, thanks to the character of Sir John Falstaff—and the new King's Men, who were now much more in demand than the Chamberlain's Men had ever been in the old reign.

In addition to the above reasons, I would add that in his Elizabethan plays the dramatist seems to be more aware, in his topicalities, of the sufferings of his persecuted fellow-Catholics, even when in certain plays he seems to be making fun of them. But in his Jacobean plays, instead of reflecting on the current religious situation—apart from the notorious example of *Macbeth* and the Gunpowder Plot—he seems to be looking more into "the dark backward and abysm" (*The Tempest* i.2) of the earlier reign of Henry VIII, when the beginning of all the troubles for Catholic England had its rise in the king's passionate desire for a divorce from the good Queen Katharine, so that he might be free to marry Anne Boleyn and perhaps beget a male heir to the throne.

This is why in the Jacobean plays we find characters such as Othello and Lear, Macbeth, Cymbeline, and Leontes, who in various ways seem to anticipate the character and actions of Henry VIII—though when that king actually appears in person in the play that bears his name, he is something of an anticlimax, like a figure in a colourful pageant wearing a fixed mask but lacking any clear characterization. As for the heroines, we may find in Desdemona and Cordelia, and even more in Hermione, so many anticipations of Katharine of Aragon, who amply matches up to expectation. Further, when we follow this line of correspondences, we may find anticipations of Anne Boleyn in "the wicked queen" of Cymbeline, who dissuades him from paying his wonted tribute to Rome, and of the Princess Mary in both Imogen and Perdita.

The main exception to all this indirect reference to Henry VIII and his marital affairs would appear to be the parallel that is occasionally drawn between Cleopatra and Elizabeth. In this I discern the dramatist's tardy response to Henry Chettle's challenge to him in *England's Mourning Garment* (1603), in which the latter complains of the unkind silence of "Melicert" when all England's other poets are vying with each other in their elegies for the passing of the great queen. Then at last, when it is safe for him to do so, Shakespeare's comes out with his backhanded compliment to Elizabeth as Cleopatra. Then he follows up *Antony and Cleopatra* with the coldly classical play of *Coriolanus*, which seems to have satisfied few critics apart from the coldly classical T. S. Eliot. And then there follows the fiery invective of *Timon of Athens*. Between them these three plays constitute a strange gap in Shakespeare's dramatic production between the two tragedies and two comedies he composed in the new reign up to 1605 and the final romances from *Pericles* (1607) onwards. Why the dramatist left such a dramatic gap, occupied by one Scottish and three "Roman" plays, is a question I hardly attempt to answer— beyond the suggestion that the impact of the Gunpowder Plot of 1605 on his dramatic inspiration may have had something to do with it.

chapter 2
Two Tragic Heroines

▨ Desdemona in *Othello*

FOR THE FIRST play to be presented in the new reign of Stuart King James I by the newly styled "King's Men", Shakespeare could hardly have made a better choice than *Othello*. One does the play an injustice by regarding it, as does A. C. Bradley, as merely the second of the so-called four great tragedies. For by comparison *Hamlet*, which comes at the tail-end of the old Elizabethan reign, is a problem play with no pretence at any *catharsis*, or tragic purification of the passions. But this is what *Othello* amply provides in the concluding murder of the heroine by the hero, who realizes the enormity of what he has done only after he has done it—and then he goes on to murder himself as well. In this way the audience can leave the theatre with a feeling of aesthetic (as opposed to moral) satisfaction!

Then, too, unlike *Hamlet*, which remains at sixes and sevens till the end, *Othello* is so well written as to fulfil all the requirements of dramatic art, while (according to Pope's ideal) "snatching a grace beyond the reach of art". Admittedly, it hardly conforms to the narrow requirements of Renaissance criticism with its emphasis on the unities of time and place, set as it is between the city of Venice and the isle of Cyprus. But once the main characters reach that isle in Act II, the dramatic time—as contrasted with the real time, which may be gauged from hints dropped here and there—seems to conform to the requirement of but a day, from the day of their arrival in Cyprus till the night when Othello kills his newly wed wife, Desdemona. All takes place so swiftly, from the moment of their clandestine marriage in Venice, by way of their arrival in Cyprus, and then from Iago's incredibly skilful temptation of Othello till its upshot in the combined murder of Desdemona and suicide of Othello. As Hopkins might have exclaimed concerning this play, "How all's to one thing wrought!"—though he is speaking "On a Piece of Music".

Here, we can't help feeling, the dramatist has put the disturbed memory of *Hamlet*—not to mention *Troilus and Cressida*—well behind him, and with the change of monarchs he has gained a new architectonic vision that may be called "Jacobean". As Mercutio exclaims of Romeo, now that his friend—all unknown to him—has changed his affections from the aloof Rosaline to the welcoming Juliet, "Now art thou Romeo!" (ii.4) So, too, may we exclaim of Shakespeare, now that he has advanced from *Hamlet* to *Othello*, "Now art thou Shakespeare!" No doubt, in *Hamlet* we see the old Elizabethan Shakespeare at his most mature, and most enigmatic, but now in *Othello* what we see is a new Jacobean Shakespeare in both the hero and the heroine, and even in the villain, as well as in the play as a whole.

Before, however, we turn to a consideration of the play as a whole, a question arises that has to be asked—though it is all too rarely asked by scholars—about this as about all the plays of Shakespeare. Namely, why did the dramatist choose this particular story, out of the hitherto untapped source of Giraldi Cinthio's *Hecatommithi*, at this particular juncture, at the beginning of the new reign? In the source Othello is called "the Moor" and Iago "the Ensign", with their setting (as also in Shakespeare's play) in Venice. And so we are reminded, as the dramatist was no doubt reminded, of an earlier Moor, the Prince of Morocco, and an earlier play set in Venice, *The Merchant of Venice*. As for Shylock and Portia, they are re-presented in the sister play of 1604, *Measure for Measure*, as the precise Angelo and the novice Isabella. After all, as he admits in his Sonnet lxxvi, Shakespeare is strangely addicted to self-repetition, writing "all one, ever the same" and keeping his "invention in a noted weed".

In that earlier play, against an Elizabethan background, the dramatist was appealing to his audience to show "the quality of mercy", and such is also the appeal he makes against the Jacobean background of *Measure for Measure*, in the inspired words of Isabella pleading for her brother before the unjust judge Lord Angelo. Portia appeals to Shylock, "We do pray for mercy, / And that same prayer doth teach us all to render / The deeds of mercy" (iv.1). So Isabella pleads with Angelo, "Why, all the souls that were, were forfeit once, / And he that might the vantage best have took, / Found out the remedy"—and that is mercy, which, as it is most divine, so its breath makes "man new made" in the image of God (ii.2). And so, too, Desdemona pleads with her stern husband for a mercy which he refuses to grant her. It may even be said that it is this biblical theme of mercy that draws the three plays together in one.

As for the three main characters, the hero, the heroine, and the villain, their respective roles are so clear-cut—unlike the *dramatis personae* in so many of Shakespeare's plays—that it even seems as if what the dramatist finds in his source is not so much the sensational murder by an over-fond husband of his newly wedded wife as the bare bones (underlying the sensational plot) of an old morality play. For here we have Othello as a black Everyman, caught in a bewildering contradiction between the ideal heroine Desdemona, who is compared to an angel, and the wicked villain Iago, who is contrarily compared to a devil. In the outcome it looks as if Othello, unlike Everyman in the mediaeval play, is destined for damnation—except that his final kiss of Desdemona, even after he has committed the further deed of self-murder, offers us hope against hope of his salvation.

What is more, the old story of the Moor and the Ensign, as retold in dramatized form by Shakespeare, receives added depth with a new and unsuspected (by the majority of Shakespeare scholars) biblical dimension. From the outset Iago appears as a self-centred traitor, concerned only with pecuniary profit—for which he shamelessly sponges on his worthless friend Roderigo, in much the same way as Sir Toby Belch sponges on Sir Andrew Aguecheek in *Twelfth Night*. Thus his typical word of advice is, "Put money enough in your purse!" (i.3). So in the story of Christ's passion, it is Judas who puts money in his purse, which he receives from the Jewish priests for the betrayal of Jesus. Iago further makes Roderigo his accomplice in the betrayal of Othello, by their revealing to Desdemona's father, Brabantio, the unsuspected loss of his dear daughter.

Then it is that the full extent of Iago's Judas-like betrayal of Othello comes to light, when Roderigo brings in Brabantio "and Officers, with torches and weapons" (i.3)—just as Judas is said in John 18:3 to bring "a band of men and officers . . . with lanterns and torches and weapons" for the apprehension of Jesus. As for Othello, like Jesus in the garden, he turns and faces his would-be captors with a calm, majestic demeanour and the dignified command, "Keep up your bright swords!"—just as Jesus told Peter on that occasion, "Put up thy sword into the sheath!" But where, it may be asked, is the kiss with which Judas betrayed his Master at this point? That kiss, we may answer, has already been mentioned by Iago to his Judas-substitute Roderigo, in his profession to "show out a flag and sign of love" (i.1). Then, too, for good measure, we may note the similar hue and cry raised by Iago at the end, against both Roderigo and Cassio, when he is recognized by his former "hit-man" as an "inhuman dog" (v.1).

As for the heroine, we may note that, if Othello appears as Christ to Iago's Judas in the first act, so Desdemona is shown in the second act in terms of the Virgin Mary—not only in the way so many of Shakespeare's heroines are depicted as "full of grace" (reminiscent of the angel's greeting in Luke i.28, in the Rheims version), but with an unprecedented degree of explicitness, presumably made possible only by the change of monarchs from the persecuting Elizabeth to the hopefully tolerant James. First, we have the gallant Cassio's welcome of her on her safe arrival in Cyprus: "Hail to thee, lady! And the grace of heaven, / Before, behind thee, and on every hand, / Enwheel thee round!" (ii.1). Secondly, we have the subsequent tempting by Iago of the demoted Cassio to seek the kind intercession of Desdemona with Othello, considering that "She is of so free, so kind, so apt, so blessed a disposition, that she holds it a vice in her goodness not to do more than she is requested" (ii.3).

Such words of praise, which Iago ironically borrows from the mouth of Roderigo (when he dismissed them with contempt), contain a clear echo of what is said in the popular prayer of the *Memorare* to the Virgin Mary attributed to St. Bernard, "Remember, O most sweet and loving Virgin Mary, that it is a thing unheard of, that anyone ever had recourse to thy protection, implored thy help, or sought thine intercession, and was left forsaken." Subsequently, when she apologizes to Cassio that now is not the time for her to make intercession with Othello on his behalf, pleading, "My advocation is not now in tune" (iii.4), her use of this unusual word (a *hapax legomenon* in Shakespeare's plays) seems to point to Mary's traditional function as "advocate of sinners", mentioned in the early mediaeval hymn, the *Salve Regina.*

By the tragic end of the play, however, while the Judas-figure of Iago changes—by way of his invocation (recalling that of Lady Macbeth, i.5) to the "divinity of hell" (ii.3)—to the "demi-devil" who has ensnared Othello's "soul and body" (v.2), the Moor has himself changed from a figure of Christ to that of Judas as a result of Iago's temptation. This change, however, he recognizes in himself only after the deed of betrayal has been done and Desdemona is dead. Then, he admits, "I were damn'd beneath all depth in hell"—with such traitors as Judas and Brutus, in Dante's *Inferno*—"But that I did proceed upon just grounds / To this extremity" (v.2)—only to find how unjust his grounds have been. He also sees himself (according to the more probable reading of "base Judean" in the Folio, as opposed to "base Indian" in the Quarto) as Judas, the only Judean among the twelve disciples, who "threw a pearl away / Richer than all his tribe"— namely, the "pearl of great price" in Christ's parable (Mt 13:46). Lastly, he recalls how, again like Judas, "I kiss'd thee ere I kill'd thee"—though now, unlike Judas, he gives Desdemona a further kiss, not of betrayal but of love and repentance, which affords us some hope of his salvation.

Then, if Othello becomes Judas on his own admission in the tragic ending of the play, to whom, we may ask, is he Judas but to his wife Desdemona? And so she becomes, in spite of her sex (which is for Shakespeare no great impediment), a figure of Christ. This figure she herself puts on in her dying words when, like Christ on the cross, she both forgives her husband for what he has done—even to the extent of denying what he has done—and commends herself to him as Christ commended himself to his Father (Lk 23:34, 46). After her death it is her handmaid Emilia who ascribes to her this figure of Christ, when she cries out at Othello, "Thou hast kill'd the sweetest innocent / That e'er did lift up eye!" In her words there is a significant combination of Judas's admission to the priests, "I have sinned betraying the innocent blood," and Pilate's protest before the people, "I am innocent of the blood of this just man" (Mt 26:4, 24). At this point Shakespeare may well have recalled the impressive sermon of Henry Smith on "The Betraying of Christ" (1594)—on which he draws more than this once—"When the innocents are betrayed, nay when the innocentest is betrayed, it seemeth more than sin, because never betrayed innocent Christ but Judas."

All this biblical reference to the story of Christ's passion, whether derived directly from a reading of the Bible or indirectly from a memory of the mystery plays, no doubt imparts to *Othello* an added depth of religious dimension—more familiar to English audiences of Shakespeare's time than to their modern counterparts. Yet there remains a further depth that makes the play not only more universal and more biblical in its hidden dimension but also more relevant to the Christian audience at the beginning of the new Jacobean age. For already in this first of his Jacobean plays we may see the dramatist looking, as Prospero tells Miranda, into "the dark backward and abysm of time" (i.2)—beyond the recent Elizabethan past of untold misery and persecution of his fellow-Catholics to the origin of their troubles in the distant reign of Henry VIII. Already in the character of Othello, with his simple conviction of Christ-like integrity and his calm assumption of regal superiority over all around him, as well as his menacing frown when once his wrath has been aroused, not least by those in whom he has placed his loving confidence, we may see early outlines of the figure of Henry.

As for the villain, who has deliberately put false suggestions into the hero's mind concerning the good faith of the heroine, one may be tempted to point an accusing finger at the person of Cardinal Wolsey, who is accused of this falsehood by Katharine herself in the play of *Henry VIII*. But it seems more likely that the dramatist was thinking of his crafty successor, Thomas Cromwell. Not that Cromwell was ever in historical fact enticing the heart of Henry away from his love for Katharine—if we see Katharine as recalled in Desdemona. But, while Desdemona is in some respects analogous to Katharine, notably in her anticipation of her tragic end, she may rather be seen as standing for the "old faith" of England, of which Katharine came to be regarded as a champion and to which Henry himself might have been called "wedded" up to the time of the divorce. In this case, Thomas Cromwell stands out as the principal minister who suggested to his royal master the Machiavellian means both of taking the divorce into his own hands, instead of waiting for a doubtful decree from Rome, and of suppressing all shrines and monasteries in the realm, so as to become the richest monarch in Christendom. From this point of view, we may well say that, if Othello is Henry, and Desdemona is Katharine, Iago is Cromwell. Once this identification is made—as it has all too rarely (if ever) been made by Shakespeare scholars—it is surprising how everything falls into place, with an almost weird precision.

Cordelia in *King Lear*

The first question to be asked about *King Lear* is why Shakespeare chose to write this play in succession to *Othello*.

The story of Lear and his three daughters would have been familiar to him from many sources—not only from his customary source in Holinshed's *Chronicles*, but also from the *Mirror for Magistrates*, Spenser's *Faery Queene,* and a recently published dramatized version of the story entitled *The True Chronicle History of King Leir*, which evidently came out in 1605. No doubt, it was partly a perceived parallel between the story of Lear and that of Othello, or rather between the characters of Desdemona in the one and Cordelia in the other, that led the dramatist to take up his pen. But he was more likely to have been prompted by indignation at the Puritan bias in the source-play, which attributes Papist tendencies to the false daughters and a Puritan mentality to Cordelia, and for this reason he decided to cut away all obvious Christian allusions from his revised version, while yet retaining a biblical content out of sight under a prudent pagan façade.

Returning then to the above-mentioned continuity with *Othello*, Lear, with his hasty temperament and his preference for the flattery of his false daughters over the plain truth of Cordelia, is close enough in character to Othello—though the punishment he metes out to Cordelia can hardly be compared in point of ferocity (except in the eyes of a Romeo) to Othello's murder of Desdemona. In any case, the sentence of banishment is contained within the limits of the opening scene, with no preceding temptation by a villain like Iago, whereas the main emphasis in *Othello* is on the great temptation scene in Act III, resulting in the murder of Desdemona in Act V. Rather, in *King Lear* it is the dramatist's aim to concentrate on the process by which the old man, who (as Regan unkindly, if truly, remarks of him) "hath ever but slenderly known himself" (i.1), grows in self-knowledge, as a result of committing himself to the care of his false daughters. And so, as Regan also observes, "To willful men, / The injuries that they themselves procure / Must be their schoolmasters" (ii.4).

As for Cordelia, her very name, as distinct from the similar sounding Cordella of the sources, has the evident meaning of *Coeur de Lear*, or "Heart of Lear"—recalling the kindred name Richard I came to bear as *Coeur de Lion*, or "Lion-heart", for his legendary heroism on the Fourth Crusade. Further, as heroine, she is the grace, or wisdom, of Lear—thus recalling the titles with which the Virgin Mary was addressed in mediaeval devotion, "Mother of Grace" and "Seat of Wisdom". So when she is banished, her place is appropriately taken by Lear's Fool, of whom she has been very fond and who is said to have "much pined him away" in her absence (i.4). This is in keeping with Shakespeare's customary alignment of heroines with fools, inasmuch as both are seen as repositories of true Christian wisdom, in contrast to the shallow wisdom of the world—according to the Erasmian ideal depicted in his *Praise of Folly*, which is in turn based on the words of St. Paul in 1 Corinthians 1. It is also significant that the Fool never appears on stage when Cordelia is present, almost as if they are conceived as one and the same person, or opposite aspects of Lear, to be played (in the dramatist's intention) by one and the same actor.

This relationship of father and daughter in *King Lear* is thus not unlike the other relationship, of husband and wife, in *Othello*, in the way they both look back to the old morality play of *Everyman*. In either case, the hero is Everyman, while the heroine is his "better angel" (to use Shakespeare's own expression in Sonnet cxliv), whom he rejects—to his own undoing. Only in *King Lear* there is no temptation by a villain like Iago, even if in the wings there are two wicked women, in the persons of the two false daughters, Goneril and Regan, waiting to take advantage of their father's folly. Hence, just as Lear in his folly has driven his good daughter into banishment, so it is now the turn of his false daughters to punish his folly by driving him into a similar banishment—sending him forth from Gloucester's castle into the storm on the heath, where there is the proverbial "grinding and gnashing of teeth".

Already, too, in the opening scene we have the three basic "moral" themes of the play represented. First, there is the theme of "Nothing", as expressed by Cordelia in reply to her father's foolish question, "What can you say to draw / A third (portion) more opulent than your sisters?" To such a question all she can truly say is "Nothing." But in his folly the old king misunderstands her and responds with the commonplace Aristotelian axiom, "Nothing will come of nothing." Whereas Cordelia's "Nothing" is born of truth and love, her father's is based on a mere calculation of words and things. In her "Nothing" Lear can recognize only an unnatural lack of filial piety, and so he unnaturally banishes her, thus showing his own lack of paternal piety. This brings us to the further theme of "Nature", which in this play refers to the relations between parents and children, according to the way (implied in the word and its derivation from the Latin verb *nasci,* "to be born") creatures are born to be. Then there is the third theme of "Self-knowledge", according to the Greek ideal of wisdom as expressed in the motto at Delphi, *Gnothi seauton,* "Know thyself". Lear's own pitiful lack of self-knowledge, in banishing his one good daughter, appears above all when he is unable to see any sign of his fatherly love in his false daughter Goneril, and he asks of those around him, "Who is it that can tell me who I am?" Then it is only the Fool who truly, if enigmatically, answers, "Lear's shadow!" (i.4).

All this is what we may learn from the dramatized story of King Lear and his three daughters, developed by Shakespeare as a morality play. But in *King Lear*, unlike *Othello*, the dramatist has added a parallel plot—not, as in other plays, a comic subplot to a serious main plot, but a secondary plot that serves to underline the events and characters of the primary plot. This other plot, featuring one of Lear's nobles, the Earl of Gloucester, and his two sons, Edgar and Edmund, Shakespeare has taken partly from Sir Philip Sidney's old pastoral romance of *Arcadia* (1590), partly from a more recent satire on Catholic exorcisms by Samuel Harsnet entitled *A Declaration of Egregious Popish Impostures* (1603). In the relation between Gloucester and his two sons there is an obvious parallel with that between Lear and his three daughters. But in Lear's case the two elder daughters are false, and only the younger is true, whereas in the case of Gloucester it is the elder son Edgar who is true and the younger bastard son Edmund who is false both to his father and to his brother—just as in *As You Like It* the place of the elder duke is usurped by his younger brother, whereas it is the elder Oliver who displaces his younger brother Orlando.

Here, too, it is the senile folly of Gloucester that inclines him to pay heed to the deceptive "Nothing" of the bastard Edmund and to drive the true Edgar from his house. Edmund's plot to dispossess his brother begins with a letter he pretends to have received from Edgar. This he hides on his father's entrance in such a way as to provoke his inquisitive father to ask what he is doing, and when he answers the expected demand with "Nothing", Gloucester responds—like Lear to Cordelia, though in another context—"Come, if it be nothing, I shall not need spectacles." Next, we are presented with another, twisted meaning of the other theme of "Nature", in Edmund's opening soliloquy, attributing to the goddess Nature that love of self which now prompts him to betray both father and brother. In his character we may recognize something of the Machiavellian villainy of Iago, as he takes a more active role in scheming against father and brother than we find in either Goneril or Regan, who merely take scheming advantage of a process set in motion by the folly of their father.

As for the minor source of Harsnet in the secondary plot, it is largely restricted to the characterization of Edgar as a mad beggar, as his way of disguising himself in order to elude the pursuit initiated by his enraged father. Then he significantly echoes the "Nothing" of Cordelia in his self-description, "Edgar I nothing am" (ii.3)—just as in *As You Like It* the exiled duke, in contrast to his younger brother Frederick, remains without a name. Incidentally, it is interesting that for this purpose the dramatist should make extended use of such a notably anti-Catholic source, which refers to a series of exorcisms conducted by a group of priests as long ago as the mid-1580s and already reflected in Shakespeare's early *Comedy of Errors*. But the account of these exorcisms, presumably by the Jesuit William Weston (whose alias was Edmonds), in a MS "Book of Miracles", had only recently come into the hands of the Bishop of London, and he entrusted Harsnet with the task of refuting the Papist exorcisms in close succession to his previous task of refuting other, Puritan exorcisms conducted in the North by John Darrell (1598–1602). For Shakespeare this material would have been interesting not only for the practical purpose of Edgar's characterization as a madman, such as the names of not a few devils, but also for the information he could gather from it concerning a former schoolmate of his from Stratford, Robert Dibdale. This Dibdale (a neighbour of Anne Hathaway's from the nearby village of Shottery) had run away from Stratford in 1575 in company with the schoolmaster Simon Hunt to become a Catholic seminarian at Douai, while Hunt went on to Rome to enter the Society of Jesus. Subsequently, Dibdale returned to England as a priest, and his services were employed by Weston for the exorcisms conducted at certain Catholic houses in the neighbourhood of London. These exorcisms were attended, among other people, by the conspirator Anthony Babington, and so Dibdale came to be implicated in the conspiracy, for which he was unjustly executed as a traitor in 1586.

The disguise adopted by Edgar as a means of escaping from pursuit is also paralleled in the primary plot, when Cordelia is accompanied into banishment by the Earl of Kent—now punished for his honesty as she for her truth. A typically blunt man, he dares to warn the old Lear of his folly in banishing his one true daughter, but he is only banished with her for his pains. At first he goes with Cordelia, proposing (like Rosalind and Celia in *As You Like It* i.3) to "shape his old course in a country new" (i.1). But he soon returns in the disguise of a servant, as a kind of spy for Cordelia, in order to enter the service of the unsuspecting Lear. Now amid his increasing troubles with his two daughters, Lear, who has begun according to the original arrangement with a retinue of a hundred knights, comes to be attended by only this one faithful (and therefore, by worldly standards, stupid) servant and the Fool. For, as the Fool remarks, only fools will follow a master in his downfall.

Now as we follow the development of the story, with Lear's increasing estrangement from his false daughters and his expulsion from their houses into the storm on the heath, we find him losing his wits and falling not only into the folly of his Fool (who, like so many of Shakespeare's fools, is a wise man turned upside-down) but also into the madness of the pretended madman Tom o' Bedlam. Then, too, we find him taking over a new biblical identity, as a Shakespearian version of the prodigal son—which the dramatist also depicts in the character of Bertram as the prodigal husband in the contemporary comedy of *All's Well That Ends Well.* Here it is the aged father who, in banishing his true daughter, has effectively banished himself into a far country, where he has wasted all his substance in frivolous behaviour, according to Goneril's true, if cruel, accusation of his having transformed "this our court" into "a riotous inn" (i.4). Now, amid the storm Kent urges him to take shelter in a poor hovel, which is recalled by Cordelia, when she returns like the merciful father in search of him. Then she exclaims, "And wast thou fain, poor father, / To hovel thee with swine and rogues forlorn, / In short and musty straw?" (iv.7). (Here the "swine" and the "straw" belong not to the play but to the parable.) In the same scene of their reunion Cordelia significantly calls Lear "this child-chang'd father", implying that he who should have been the father in the parable has been changed into the prodigal son, and "poor perdu", or lost one, in that, like the prodigal son, "he was lost, but he is found" (Lk 15:31).

Secondly, amid the pitiless storm Lear is reduced to the miserable condition not only of the prodigal son in the far country, but also of Job in the Old Testament. Much as he continually urges himself to be patient, according to the "pattern" of Job proposed by St. James in his epistle (5:11), he may still be compared to Job in his impatience, not just at the ingratitude of his false daughters but also at the widespread injustice in the society of his (and Shakespeare's) time. In such a society, he complains, the "small vices" of beggars appear all too openly through their "tatter'd clothes", whereas "Robes and furr'd gowns hide all" (iv.6). Also like Job, who complains even of divine injustice, Lear maintains, "I am a man / More sinn'd against than sinning" (iii.2). The very image of the storm in the Gentleman's description, "Wherein the cub-drawn bear would couch, / The lion and the belly-pinched wolf / Keep their fur dry" (iii.1), seems to echo the mention in Job of such weather, when "the beasts go into the den and remain in their places" (37:8).

Thirdly, all these sufferings of Lear, whether drawn from Job in the Old Testament or from the prodigal son in the New, increasingly point to those of Christ himself in his passion and death on the cross—familiar to Shakespeare as well from the mystery plays he could have witnessed at Coventry in his boyhood as from his experience of the liturgy of Holy Week and his personal reading of the Bible. In connection not only with Lear himself, but also with the other old man Gloucester, as well as their two helpers in disguise, Kent and Edgar, it is noticeable how in the last few scenes of this truly "impassioned" play there is a succession of what Edgar calls "side-piercing" sights (iv.6). Such a sight is the meeting of the two old men, the one maddened by the ingratitude of his two false daughters and the other blinded in consequence of his wicked son's treachery, and another is the coming on stage of the grief-crazed father with the dead body of his innocent daughter—as it were recalling the piercing of the side of Christ on the cross by a soldier with his lance (Jn 19:34). Then it is that Kent exclaims, on witnessing the heartbroken death of his royal master, "Break, heart, I prithee, break!" There are, strangely enough, scholars who refuse to recognize any sign of Christianity in such a heartrending tragedy, and yet that is what Christianity, not least in the story of the passion and death of Christ on the cross, is all about!

As the play of *King Lear* draws to an end, we may notice, as at the end of *Othello*, a veritable explosion of biblical reference that aptly serves to explode the scepticism of atheistic or agnostic commentators. It is all too often alleged that Christianity promises a reward even in this life for virtuous deeds, and Jesus himself may be quoted to this effect in reply to his disciples on what they may expect from their discipleship (Mt 19:29). But what he more frequently and characteristically promises to his followers is the way of the cross, which he himself is the first to tread. That way, which is seen as culminating in his passion and death, is shown in *King Lear* as leading on to the sufferings and deaths of both Lear and Cordelia, not to mention Gloucester. Of the two, however, it is Cordelia rather than Lear who is presented to us in the figure of Christ. Even from the outset, when she is welcomed in her abjection by the King of France, she is all but explicitly compared to Christ as Man of Sorrows: "Fairest Cordelia, that art most rich, being poor, / Most choice, forsaken, and most lov'd, despis'd" (i.1). So Christ is said by St. Paul, though rich as Son of God, to have become poor (2 Cor 8:9). He is called the "chosen" servant by Isaiah (49:3), and yet "forsaken" by God (Ps 22:1), and as Man of Sorrows he is "despised and rejected of men" (Is 53:3). Subsequently, when she returns in search of her wandering father, she makes her own the words of the child Jesus to his mother in the temple, "O dear father! / It is thy business that I go about" (iv.4, cf. Luke 2:49). Then, when a Gentleman is sent to find her father and bring him to her tent, he tells Lear, "Thou hast one daughter, / Who redeems nature from the general curse / Which twain have brought her to." His words are a strange misfit in their dramatic context, but they are a tissue of texts from St. Paul (1 Tim 2:5–6, Tit 2:14, Gal 3:13).

Paradoxically, this configuration of Cordelia with Christ appears not so much in her blissful reunion with Lear—save insofar as her response to his recognition of her, "And so I am, I am" (iv.7), seems to echo the divine name as revealed to Moses, "I am who I am" (Ex 3:14)—as in the sorrowful ending of Act V. Then she is killed by hanging, as though with reference to the hanging of Christ on the cross. And then she is brought on stage by her grieving father, as though in a dramatic replica of the *Pieta*. This tableau of the sorrowing parent holding the dead body of his innocent child is indeed recognized in terms of the *Pieta* by not a few Shakespeare scholars, especially in view of the excited exclamation of Albany, "O see, see!" Then he all but echoes the words of Jeremiah in his Lamentations, "Behold and see, if there be any sorrow like unto my sorrow!" (Lam 1:12)— words that are explicitly applied to the *Pieta* in the Church's liturgy for Holy Week. It is as if the whole point of *King Lear* in the dramatist's intention is to represent this climactic moment in the passion of Christ (though not recorded in any of the Gospels) in such a way as to remind the audience of this central mystery of the Christian faith in an unexpected manner and so to shock them into recognition.

That, however, isn't all there is to be said about the deep meaning of *King Lear*, once we apply to this play the same meta-dramatic principle we applied to *Othello*. Rather, the profound pull it makes on the audience's heartstrings is to be attributed not just to the pitiful tale of Lear and Cordelia, nor only to the biblical story of the passion and death of Christ, but also to the deep relevance of it all to the contemporary sufferings of Catholics in Tudor England. From this topical viewpoint, who may Lear be supposed to represent but that lion among English kings, Henry VIII? What with his separation from Rome owing to his desire of a divorce from Katharine of Aragon and of a second marriage with Anne Boleyn, and his subsequent spoliation of all shrines and monasteries in the realm, he effectively banished the

Catholic faith from England and entrusted himself to the care of such Lutheran sympathizers as Anne Boleyn, Thomas Cranmer, and Thomas Cromwell. Then Cordelia may be seen, like Desdemona, as reflecting the character of Katharine, at least insofar as the latter stood for the Catholic faith and unity with Rome. And so in her pitiful death, as in that of Desdemona, we may hear the lament of the dramatist himself over the passing of Catholic England.

On the other hand, when we turn to such lesser characters as Kent, who returns from France under the guise of a servant, and Edgar, who stays in the country under the guise of a mad beggar, we may see in them types of the hunted priest in Elizabethan England. From the time of Edmund Campion in 1580, and even before, it was death for any priest ordained beyond the seas and returning to England to minister to his fellow-countrymen. So he had to resort to such forms of disguise in order to avoid arrest, imprisonment, torture, and death as a traitor, by being hanged, drawn, and quartered. Edgar in particular seems to invite such a comparison, not only because of his characterization based on Harsnet's *Declaration*, but also because of the way proclamations are published against him, ports are guarded to apprehend him, and intelligence (from spies and informers) is given against him (ii.1,3)—all of them technical terms applied to Catholic priests in Elizabethan England, but quite anachronistic of Lear's Britain.

If we may carry these topical correspondences even further, if more conjecturally, to whom may we compare the false daughters of Lear but to Elizabeth herself—as we may also recognize her in such subsequent characters as Lady Macbeth and Cleopatra? Cornwall may then be recognized in the Earl of Leicester, especially in his words of commendation to Edmund, "Natures of such deep trust we shall much need" (ii.1)—recalling the patronage extended to the young Edmund Campion during the latter's brilliant career at Oxford, and perhaps even suggesting the choice of that name to the dramatist's mind.

Lastly, the pseudo-Chaucerian prophecy which the Fool attributes to Merlin concerning the state of Britain, "When priests are more in word than matter . . . / Then shall the realm of Albion / Come to great confusion" (iii.2), is interestingly quoted by several Catholic authors in the 1590s, such as Richard Verstegan in the preface to his *Declaration of the True Causes* (1592), and specifically applied by them to the contemporary condition of their country. Above all, the ravings of Lear against the injustices of the time, which go far beyond any immediate relevance to his false daughters, are only too true of the situation in Elizabethan England, as described (for example) by Robert Southwell in his *Humble Supplication to Her Majesty* (1600), where he laments, "We are made the common theme of every railing declaimer, abused without hope or means of remedy, by every wretch with most infamous names, no tongue so forsworn but it is of credit against us, none so true but it is thought false in our defence. . . . So heavy is the hand of our superiors against us, that we generally are accounted men whom it is a credit to pursue, a disgrace to protect, a commodity to spoil, a gain to torture, and a glory to kill."

chapter 3
Two Problematic Heroines

Isabella in *Measure for Measure*

Here I have to begin with a word of protest against the common attachment of the epithet "problem" to the first two comedies of Shakespeare in the Jacobean age, *Measure for Measure* and *All's Well That Ends Well*. There is all the difference in the world between the two properly called "problem" tragedies at the end of the Elizabethan age, *Hamlet* and *Troilus and Cressida*, and these two Jacobean comedies, whose problem is more in the minds of those critics who pick bones in them than in the plays themselves. The only real problem I am disposed to admit in them is the lack of a suitable hero to match the heroine. In either case the heroine is the character who really stands out in the list of *dramatis personae*, while we are left wondering as to who is really the hero.

From the outset of *Measure for Measure* we notice the similarity in its main plot to the Elizabethan *Merchant of Venice*—with Isabella recalling the lady Portia, Lord Angelo Shylock the Jew, and the Duke-Friar Vincentio-Lodowick the merchant Antonio. There, too, Portia is clearly the heroine, corresponding to Isabella, but Shylock, like Angelo, however vividly characterized, is more villain than hero. As for Antonio, he may be Shylock's victim, above all in the trial scene, but that hardly makes him the hero of the play, and his young friend Bassanio is too lightly drawn as a character to qualify him as hero—though he may be given the credit for winning the lady Portia. In this play it is perhaps Vincentio, both as duke and as friar, who has a better claim to be accepted as hero—like Prospero, with whom he is often compared, in *The Tempest*. But his part, like that of Friar Laurence (even if combined with that of the Prince) in *Romeo and Juliet*, is too subordinate to the welfare of the lovers, Claudio and Juliet, for a hero—even if he does propose to Isabella, in his capacity as duke, at the end.

Another peculiar characteristic of *Measure for Measure* among the plays of Shakespeare is its openly biblical title, derived from Christ's words in his Sermon on the Mount, "With what measure ye mete, it shall be measured to you again" (Mt 7:2). Such a serious title, which is also echoed in the text and even intoned by the duke in the final scene, "Like doth quit like, and measure still for measure" (v.1), stands in significant contrast to the triviality of the titles given by the weary dramatist to three of his last comedies in the Elizabethan age. It even looks as if he has been "born again" into the new reign as a convert to Puritanism, but for the fact that the whole tendency of the play is directed against the Puritans in the person of "the precise Angelo" (i.3, iii.1)—just as the tendency of *The Merchant of Venice* may be seen as directed against the same Puritans as represented by Shylock. It may further be noted that the dramatist continues the same proverbial form of title in his choice for the next comedy of *All's Well That Ends Well*, whose title is twice echoed in the text with a similar kind of intonation (iv.4, v.1).

What makes the two comedies seem problematic in the eyes of not a few modern critics is perhaps the way both heroines resort to a "bed-trick" for the solution to their problems—though it is a very different kind of problem from what we find in either of the late Elizabethan tragedies. In *Measure for Measure* Isabella is persuaded by the duke-friar, whom she knows as Friar Lodowick, to cooperate in this plan of his as a means of saving her from the sexual advances of the unjust judge Angelo, besides saving the life of her condemned brother Claudio. She merely pretends to agree to Angelo's proposal, while substituting Angelo's former betrothed, "Mariana of the Moated Grange" (who has the right to share his bed by reason of their "pre-contract"— the very situation for which Claudio and Juliet are being punished). In *All's Well That Ends Well* it is the heroine Helena herself who persuades the chaste Diana to accept the sexual advances of Bertram, while she proposes to take Diana's place in bed that night, that she may get a child by her husband, according to the condition he has laid down for their reconciliation.

What is more, in either case the trick is justified with an appeal to something like "equivocation"—the moral expedient resorted to by English Jesuits at that time, so as to escape incriminating themselves or others when subjected to interrogation (often with the use of torture) by the authorities. In the former play, the duke-friar, who is himself, though professedly a Franciscan, yet a kind of Jesuit in disguise, declares, "So disguise shall, by the disguis'd / Pay with falsehood false exacting" (iii.2). In the latter, Diana says in deciding to follow Helena's advice, "Only in this disguise I think't no sin / To cozen him that would unjustly win" (iv.2). Even Jesuit moralists might have had reservations about such reasoning!

We turn now to Isabella, and especially to her name: it is not to be found in any of the suggested sources of the play, where she is named Epitia in the one and Cassandra in the other—while in neither is she shown as a novice. Rather, it is evidently derived from a possible relative of the dramatist's, Isabella Shakespeare, who had been prioress of Wroxhall Abbey in the Forest of Arden before the Reformation—where there had been yet another nun named Joanna Shakespeare. One reason for this choice of name is that Isabella is here characterized as a novice applying for admission into a convent of Poor Clares, or what she herself calls "the sisterhood, the votarists of Saint Clare" (i.4), while the duke, in absenting himself from the cares of his dukedom, correspondingly applies for acceptance as a Franciscan friar (i.3). Such a strongly Catholic flavour at the very beginning of the play must surely have come to the adverse attention of an Elizabethan censor, but now at the beginning of the new reign, when he himself was in high favour at court, the dramatist would have got away with it. As for the mysterious "Mariana of the Moated Grange" (iii.1, iv.1), there happens to be such a moated grange at Baddesly Clinton in the neighbourhood of Wroxhall Abbey, which we know was used in Elizabethan times as a secret meeting-place for English Jesuits, and which fits in very well with the detailed description of Mariana's trysting-place with Angelo (iv.1).

For these and other reasons there is something unique about *Measure for Measure* as being the most openly religious and even Catholic of all Shakespeare's plays. In the opinion of Christopher Devlin, "it is the only great religious play that has graced the English stage between the Middle Ages and T. S. Eliot", and "it is a great Christian play worked out in terms of explicitly Roman Catholic, Papist symbols" (*Hamlet's Divinity*, 27). In the previous reign of Elizabeth drama had to be secular, owing to a prohibition issued early on in the reign against the use of plays for religious propaganda. Even so, it may be said that in *The Merchant of Venice* the dramatist is sailing close to the wind, considering that it has something of a religious, even controversial, aspect in the confrontation between Jews and Christians, as between the Old and the New Testament—and implicitly between Puritans and Papists. It is this aspect that fills the play with biblical echoes, most of them coming from the mouth of Shylock, who is no less well read in the New than in the Old Testament. Still, it might have been excused as a sequel to Marlowe's *Jew of Malta* (1589), in connection with the contemporary scandal involving Roderigo Lopez, the queen's Jewish physician, who had been accused of trying to poison her. From this point of view, *Measure for Measure* might in turn be regarded as Shakespeare's sequel to his own *Merchant of Venice*, only the topical contrast of the Catholic novice versus the Puritan judge is dangerously explicit.

In the main plot Lord Angelo, who has been entrusted by Duke Vincentio with the administration of law in Vienna during the other's absence, is depicted as a strict interpreter of "the old law", which forbids the sin of fornication under pain of death. He is, moreover, described as "precise" (i.3), which was then the characteristic epithet attached to the Puritans, "the precise brethren". His reputation is tested in the first case brought to his attention, concerning a young couple, Isabella's brother, Claudio, and his girlfriend, Juliet, who have been caught in the act of fornication—though the sin is attenuated in their case by the fact that they are betrothed to each other in a "pre-contract". This was accepted in Elizabethan England as a common-law marriage once it had been consummated, and (as we have seen) it is later shown in the play as already existing between Angelo himself and Mariana. Yet even for this sin, confessed as such

by both Claudio and Juliet, the old law of Vienna decrees
the death penalty—recalling the similar penalty attaching to
adultery in the law of Moses (Lev 20:10), which the Puritans, following their leader Thomas Cartwright, regarded as
still applying to Christians under the new law of Christ.

As for the duke-friar, whose name as duke is Vincentio
and as friar is Lodowick, he is a masterful character, anticipating Prospero, the former Duke of Milan in *The Tempest*,
both of whom are seen as masks for the dramatist himself.
From the beginning he is introduced to us as retiring for a
while from the affairs of his duchy, so as to test the seeming
virtue of Lord Angelo, while he returns in disguise as a Franciscan friar. Now as friar, with the understanding of the
other friars in Vienna (so he can't be said to be "masquerad-
ing" as one), he purposes to "visit the afflicted spirits . . . in
the prison" (ii.3)—recalling the words in which Christ is
described by St. Peter as visiting the imprisoned spirits in
the underworld after his death on the cross, in what is tradi-
tionally known as "the harrowing of hell" (1 Pet 3:19). In
particular, he visits Claudio and Juliet in their separate pris-
ons and brings them comfort, not only with words of advice
similar to the counsel given by Friar Francis to Hero in
Much Ado About Nothing, "Die to live!" (iv.1), but also by
devising practical measures on their behalf. With them he
thus concludes a practical syllogism formed by the names of
lovers assisted by the three friars in Shakespeare's plays,
Romeo and Juliet, Claudio and Hero, Claudio and Juliet.

Using the sacred power conferred on him not only by his
"bless'd order" as a friar (ii.3) but also, as he claims, "in special business from his holiness", the Pope (iii.2), Friar
Lodowick shows his resourcefulness in resorting to a variety
of stratagems—reminiscent of that "polypragmon" or busy-
body (as his enemies called him), the Jesuit Robert Persons.

He first teaches Juliet "how you shall arraign your con-science", in order to make a true confession of her sins, draw-ing on the moralists' distinction between true penitence based on love and that which is "hollowly put on" (ii.3), as based on fear—or, in technical terms, between contrition and attrition. In another prison-cell he further exhorts Clau-dio to face his sentence of death with resignation, by being "absolute for death" (iii.1). He so convinces the young man that the other declares, "To sue to live, I find I seek to die, / And seeking death, find life" (iii.1). Here we may recognize another echo of the above-mentioned advice of Friar Francis in *Much Ado About Nothing*, "Die to live!" (iv.1), as well as a poem by the Jesuit martyr Robert Southwell, "I live, but such a life as ever dies. / I die, but such a death as never ends. / . . . My living death by dying life is fed."

Such a play is indeed the most religious, even Catholic, of all Shakespeare's plays—despite its bawdy content, which may well have been the reason why yet another Jesuit in Val-ladolid, William Sankey, was prompted to delete the whole play in his censorship of the Second Folio of 1632 on behalf of the Spanish Inquisition. What with the heroine as a novice, the duke as a friar, and the villain as a precisian or Puritan, the implied message could hardly have been clearer. Yet scholars still quibble over its meaning with their natura-listic presuppositions, applying to it the requirements of modern realism, which incline them to shut their eyes to the subject of religion—unless treated with sarcasm and satire.

There is, however, less of a problem among those who interpret the play, as its title seems to require, in terms of a mediaeval morality play, such as the fifteenth-century *Castle of Perseverance*. This centres on a dispute among the four daughters of God, Mercy and Truth, Peace and Justice, fea-tured in Psalm 85, over the redemption of Man, in view of the conflicting claims of Justice and Mercy. In *Measure for Measure* it is Angelo who, like the English Puritans, insists on applying the law in all its rigour especially against the Papists, whereas it is Isabella who, as a Catholic novice, stands (like Portia) for the ideal of Mercy not only for her brother Claudio (ii.2) but even for the unjust Angelo, once he has been convicted of his injustice (v.1). As for the duke-friar, he is recognized by Angelo in the outcome of the play in terms of divine providence: "I perceive your grace, like power divine, / Hath look'd upon my passes" (v.1).

In this outcome a further problem is raised by the above-mentioned critics concerning the duke's repeated proposal of marriage to Isabella, to which she makes no reply. This is not only a theoretical problem for critics but also a practical problem for producers, who have to decide how to depict the response of Isabella, whether as accepting or rejecting the proposal. Theoretically, Isabella's acceptance might imply a turning back on that religious life which has been so much admired in her by the licentious Lucio: "I hold you as a thing ensky'd and sainted, / By your renouncement an immortal spirit, / And to be talk'd with in sincerity, / As with a saint" (i.4). Practically, her rejection of the proposal might be taken to show a distaste for all the stratagems pursued by the duke-friar, and implicitly for the activities of the Jesuits at that time. But for those who admit an allegorical interpretation of the play, such as was still acceptable till well on into the seventeenth century, there is no great problem. Once the duke is seen as standing for divine providence and Isabella for divine mercy, the heroine may well take his hand and let him lead her offstage for the expected happy ending of a Shakespearian comedy.

Then, it may be asked, what about a further meta-dramatic dimension to this play? Already we have noticed more than a little of its moral and biblical dimension, not least in its ending, when an allegorical meaning seems to be demanded in spite of the requirements of naturalistic critics. Here, in addition to the biblical title from the Sermon on the Mount, we may notice the parable of a ruler going on a long journey and leaving his servants with various "talents" till the time of his return (Mt 25:14–30), the episode of the woman taken in adultery (Jn 8:1–11), as well as the conflicting claims of justice and mercy implied in Psalm 85 and developed in the old morality play. Then, beyond this pervasive biblical dimension, there is the topical dimension of reference to the situation of Catholics in the past Elizabethan age, centring on the contrast between the Catholic novice, with the assistance of the Franciscan friar, and the Puritan judge. Here, as suggested above, the devious "indirections" of the friar (cf. *Hamlet* ii.2) point not so much to the Franciscans, of whom there were few in England at that time, as to the Jesuits, who are described by their archenemy Lord Burghley, in his *Execution of Justice in England* (1583), as wandering "up and down in corners, in disguised sort"—much as the duke is described by Lucio as "the old fantastical duke of dark corners" (iv.3).

Finally, in the case of the "pre-contract" which extenuates the fornication of Claudio and Juliet, while bringing them under the penalty of the law, as interpreted by the Puritan judge, there may perhaps be an echo of the marital arrangement between William Shakespeare and Anne Hathaway in 1582. Insofar as they must have sought a Catholic wedding, to be celebrated in the bride's church at Temple Grafton by the old Marian priest Sir John Frith, possibly in the summer of that year, they were going against the laws of the Anglican Church. Then, once Anne was seen to be big with child, it was imperative for them to have their wedding legally recog-

nized by obtaining the required licence from the diocesan
registry office at Worcester for exemption from the necessary banns during the season of Advent. And that is what
they secured in the late November of 1582, when the clerk
made the notorious mix-up between the two Annes, Hathaway and Whateley, of whom the latter is designated as "of
Temple Grafton". Thus not only the names of Isabella as a
Catholic novice and Mariana of the Moated Grange as
pointing to Baddesly Clinton, but also the "pre-contract" of
Claudio and Juliet together point to an intimate connection
between this play as a whole—in this respect not unlike the
earlier Elizabethan comedy of *As You Like It*—and the personal life and beliefs of the dramatist.

Helena in *All's Well That Ends Well*

No less central than the place of Isabella in the comedy of
Measure for Measure is that of Helena in the subsequent comedy of *All's Well That Ends Well*. From the beginning she is
introduced to us as an orphan, daughter of a famous doctor,
Gerard de Narbon, and now she is living at the court of
Rousillon, where she has been brought up with the young
Count Bertram, who is without a father but under the care
of his mother, the Countess. Helena has fallen in love with
him, but he has no interest in her. When he is summoned to
the court of the French king at Paris, she resolves to follow
him, bringing with her a special remedy left her by her father,
with which she hopes to cure the king of a seemingly incur-
able illness. The remedy proves to be so successful that it is
hailed as a miracle, and by way of reward she is told by the
king to choose whatever reward she desires. All she desires is
the hand of Count Bertram in marriage, and he is obliged by
the king to take her as his wife. On the night of their marriage, however, the young man runs away to join the war in

Florence, while she follows him in disguise as a pilgrim—not unlike the other Helena who follows Demetrius in *A Midsummer Night's Dream*. On her arrival in Florence, she meets a chaste girl named Diana, who is being wooed as a lover by Bertram, and she persuades Diana to pretend acceptance of his sexual advances, while she takes the place of the girl in bed with him that night. Thus she is enabled to conceive a child of Bertram's, in accordance with his condition that there can be no reunion between them until she presents him with a child of theirs.

All in all, it is a strange story for Shakespeare to have chosen for dramatization, and it has puzzled not a few commentators, who are undecided where and how to fit it into the dramatist's *oeuvre* as a whole—especially as there was no record of a performance of the play in Shakespeare's lifetime (and not till 1741), nor any text of the play before the First Folio of 1623. Yet it has many points, as already noticed, in parallel with *Measure for Measure*, such as its proverbial title and the plot of the "bed-trick". Further, what few scholars recognize is that the play takes its point of departure not only from a source in Boccaccio's *Decameron*, translated into English in William Painter's *Palace of Pleasure* (1567), but also from two contemporary controversies which combine to indicate a date of 1605.

One was a controversy which arose out of a claim made in 1604 by the town-clerk of Brussels, Philip Numan, about certain miracles being worked at two shrines of Our Lady in the nearby towns of Halle and Montaigu—a controversy that was taken up on the Catholic side by the humanist Justus Lipsius in 1604 and 1605, and soon spread across the Channel to England. The other was a medical controversy between the orthodox Galenist physicians (who looked up to the medical authority of the Greek Galen) and the Paracelsian newcomers (who followed the methods prescribed by the contemporary Platonist Paracelsus), arising out of the contemporary plague afflicting Londoners in the early years of the new reign. These two controversies might well explain why the story of Boccaccio came to the attention of the dramatist at this time, as well as its parallel with his recent comedy of *Measure for Measure*. What is more, the emphasis laid on the character of Helena, not to mention her change of name (as in the case of Isabella), over any other character in the play seems to point unmistakably to the former of the controversies, on the miracles said to have been wrought at the intercession of Our Lady.

Here we pass almost at once from the dimension of drama to that of meta-drama, and from the character of Helena to the figure of Our Lady behind her. From the time of her appearance at the French court, she justifies her proposed attempt to cure the king by claiming, "He that of greatest works is finisher / Oft does them by the weakest minister" (ii.1)—as it were echoing Mary's words in her hymn of praise known as the *Magnificat*, "He that is mighty hath done for me great things, and holy is his name" (Lk 1:49). She goes on to attribute her medicinal power not to herself or her father but to "the great'st grace lending grace". Convinced by her inspired words, the king replies in a similar vein, "Methinks in thee some blessed spirit doth speak / His powerful sound within an organ weak." In the outcome the courtier Lord Lafeu exclaims in amazement, "They say miracles are past", whereas now he cannot help wondering at this "showing of a heavenly effect in an earthly actor" and "in a most weak and debile minister, great transcendence" (ii.3). The audience, of course, knows that this is all attributable to the remedy entrusted to Helena by her gifted father, but the emphasis laid in the play on this seeming miracle, in contrast to those rationalists who say that "miracles are past", evidently refers to the contemporary controversy in which it was the Anglican position, as earlier stated by the Archbishop of Canterbury in *Henry V*, that "miracles are ceas'd" (i.1).

The plot of *All's Well That Ends Well*, both as drama and as meta-drama, may be seen, moreover, as divided into two parts, with Helena first as miracle-worker and then as pilgrim—in either case, no less than the plot of *Measure for Measure*, from a clearly Catholic viewpoint. In her search for her wayward husband Bertram, it is significant that Helena adopts the guise of a pilgrim to the Spanish shrine of St. James at Compostela—though her route from Rousillon to Florence is oddly devious. In this guise she follows the example of previous lovers in Shakespeare's plays—not only Julia in *Two Gentlemen of Verona* and her own namesake in *A Midsummer Night's Dream*, but also (in point of language) Romeo and Juliet in the first scene of their meeting (i.5), followed by Bassanio and the Prince of Morocco in their wooing of Portia in *The Merchant of Venice* (i.1, ii.7). Her very name, too, the dramatist has altered from the original Giletta to that of St. Helena, mother of the emperor Constantine and the first Christian pilgrim, noted in mediaeval legend for her pilgrimage to Jerusalem in search of the true cross of Christ.

At the same time, in the character of Bertram, as of King Lear, there is more than a suggestion of Christ's parable of the prodigal son. First, we are shown the way Helena goes in search of her straying husband, as Cordelia returns from France in search of her straying father. Then, too, we are shown the anxiety of the old Countess as she shakes her head over her son, demanding, "What angel shall / Bless this unworthy husband?" (iii.4). The "angel" to whom she refers is obviously Helena, as being Bertram's wife, of whom she goes on to say, "He cannot thrive, / Unless her prayers, whom heaven delights to hear, / And loves to grant, reprieve him from the wrath / Of greatest justice." Though in terms of the plot the Countess is here speaking of Helena, her words are hardly to be explained—as in the above cases of Desdemona and Isabella—without reference to the Virgin Mary as advocate of sinners, a title we have specially noted as occurring in the liturgical hymn *Salve Regina.* Thus it may be safely claimed that, both as worker of miracles and as pilgrim, Helena looks to the Virgin Mary.

chapter 4

The Lady and No Lady

The Lady in *Macbeth*

MACBETH IS INDEED, for all its popularity, a strange play. Rated though it is among the "great" tragedies of Shakespeare, it shares the distinction, with *The Comedy of Errors*, of being his shortest play. Even so, there are scenes which clamour to be cut. That of Hecate and the witches (iii.5) is obviously spurious and is attributed, not without reason, to Thomas Middleton, and that between Malcolm and Macduff (iv.3) is unnecessarily long and even tedious. The play is commonly dated in the year 1606, on account of the reference in the Porter scene (ii.3) to the trials of the Gunpowder plotters earlier that year. Yet it also looks back to the aftermath of the Essex rebellion of 1601 and the composition of *Hamlet*, when Shakespeare with some of his fellows in the Chamberlain's Men may have visited Edinburgh and entertained King James VI. It also looks as if the dramatist had a mind to present it at court for the further entertainment of the new King James I, who claimed Banquo among his ancestors and whose *Daemonologie* (1597) seems to be echoed in the play. But then it would have had to be postponed on account of the plague raging in London soon after James's accession to the throne. For these reasons—as

well as the known aversion of James to long plays—it may
be said that *Macbeth* is a "patched-up job". And that may
explain why it was never printed in quarto form in Shakespeare's lifetime, but its first appearance in print was in the
First Folio of 1623.

Not only in the play of *Macbeth* but also in the hero
there is this quality of strangeness. For in himself—as it
were following in the footsteps of Richard III—he combines
the contrary roles of hero and villain. Even from the beginning he is by no means the brave, loyal general he is sometimes made out to be. Rather, he is shown as a man of
blood, delighting "to bathe in reeking wounds" and intent
on memorizing "another Golgotha" (i.2)—like those mentioned in the letter to the Hebrews who "crucify again to
themselves the Son of God and make a mock of him" (6:6).
So when the three witches prompt in him thoughts of ambition, even by taking the way of blood, it is evidently not the
first time such thoughts have occurred to him or his lady.
Nor is it long before his Judas-like treachery appears, for all
his poetic piety. Then from his identification with Judas it
isn't long before a further identity appears in him—as in the
case of Iago—as a figure of Satan.

Thus, whereas in *Othello* we are left with a final gleam of
hope for the hero's salvation, through the intercession of
Desdemona whose dying prayer was for him, in *Macbeth*
there is no such hope for the hero. Rather, in contrast to
Othello, *Macbeth* may even be described as "a morality play
of damnation". In this respect, the hero is explicitly contrasted with the previous Thane of Cawdor, to whose title he
succeeds, and who is said to have died after setting forth "A
deep repentance"—at which news Duncan makes the
unconsciously ironical remark, "There's no art / To find the
mind's construction in the face" (i.4). Here the king is refer-

ring to the thane who has just been executed for treason, but he little realizes—with the innocence born of ignorance—that the succeeding thane is to become even more of a traitor.

A main reason why Macbeth is deprived of any hope of salvation is that in this play the villain is not only the hero but also the heroine, who in other circumstances might be expected to have been his "better angel"—like Desdemona to Othello. For Lady Macbeth at least in the first two acts is even the "worser spirit" (Sonnet cxliv) of her husband, who, she complains, is "too full o' the milk of human kindness" (i.5). It isn't just that she has been tempted from his side, but she has herself already yielded to temptation with her fearful appeal—all too reminiscent of Iago's invocation of the "divinity of hell" (ii.3)—to the "spirits / That tend on mortal thoughts" to "unsex me here, / And fill me from the crown to the toe top full / Of direst cruelty" (i.5). In one sense she may be called a fit partner to Macbeth, but in another sense she is so fit to him in his villainy as to preclude any possibility of repentance in him. Romantic interpreters may like to see them as lovers, though in crime, but whatever love there may have been between them earlier on—as when Macbeth calls her "dearest chuck" (iii.2)—is shown as steadily fading while the villain proceeds from crime to crime, leaving his wife in the innocence of ignorance. In any case, for all the greatness she exhibits in the first two acts, and for all her strong femininity—in contrast to her prayer to be unsexed—she makes less of an overall impression than her more poetic, if villainous, husband.

By contrast with the evil represented in both hero and heroine, the ideal of divine grace, normally reserved by Shakespeare for the heroine, is shown in a succession of three kings, who are "gracious" not just in virtue of their royalty but also of that "divinity" which, as Claudius fondly imagines, "doth hedge a king" (*Hamlet* iv.5). First comes "the gracious Duncan"—as he is named by his very murderer (iii.1)—who is made by the dramatist into far more gracious a figure than the historical Scottish king of that name. Then there is the saintly Edward King of England, concerning whom Malcolm says that "sundry blessings hang about his throne / That speak him full of grace" (iv.3). It is largely thanks to the support of Edward that Malcolm with Macduff is enabled to overthrow the usurper in Scotland, and once they have achieved the victory, Malcolm takes over from the wise rule of his royal father, with the proposal to rule "by the grace of grace"—as it were through an accumulation of grace.

As for the plotting of the play, it is in one sense exceedingly simple—uncomplicated by any secondary plot as in *King Lear*—with a main plot that runs through the whole play with single-minded intensity, like that of *Othello* poetically compared to the "icy current" of the Pontic Sea, which "keeps due on / To the Propontic and the Hellespont" (iii.3). Only, whereas in *Othello* there is but one contrived murder, that of the poor heroine, in *Macbeth* there is a succession of murders, beginning with that of Duncan in Act II, then going on to the further murder of Banquo in Act III, followed by that of Lady Macduff and her children in Act IV—not to mention the innumerable victims of Macbeth's blood-lust vaguely mentioned by Malcolm and Macduff as well as Ross (iv.3). Here it is noteworthy that not only does one sin pluck on another by a kind of fatality, but in each of these successive murders one alone is killed while another escapes to prepare the path of divine vengeance. So while Duncan is murdered, his two sons Malcolm and Donalbain make their escape. Banquo is murdered, but his son Fleance escapes. Lady Macduff and her children are murdered, but her husband, Macduff, has already escaped to the court of Edward in England, where he proceeds to join forces with Malcolm and Edward against Macbeth. Thus everything in this play, as in the previous history play of *Richard III*, leads up to the final act of vengeance, with an evil ending for Macbeth and his lady but a good ending— all too often overlooked by those who are romantically mesmerized by the hero-villain—for Scotland.

Abstractly speaking, the plotting of the play may seem to be well balanced, according to the symmetrical, Euclidian ideal of Renaissance criticism, but the general impression left by the play is unbalanced. The memorable scenes are all crammed into the first two acts, in which the hero-villain at the instigation first of the witches, then of his wife, kills the gracious king, and the deed is discovered, but not the doer. What follows, however, seems like a succession of cover-ups—as if in anticipation of the detective stories of Agatha Christie—while the humanity of both villains, husband and wife, declines into that world-weariness which is expressed so splendidly by the hero on learning of his wife's death, in his soliloquy, "Tomorrow, and tomorrow, and tomorrow" (v.5). There remain only two gleams of their former greatness, first in the sleep-walking scene of Lady Macbeth, followed by the news of her death—as we learn only at the end, "as 'tis thought, by self and violent hands" (v.7)—and secondly in the last stand taken by Macbeth, as he desperately defends the besieged castle, preferring rather to die in the harness of a soldier than to "play the Roman fool" (like Cassius and Brutus at the end of *Julius Caesar*).

All this dramatization of Scottish history, in Shakespeare's adaptation of Holinshed's *Chronicles* to purposes of his own, receives a deeper dimension from all the Christian and biblical references with which this play is more than usually charged. It even seems as if the dramatist is enjoying a "last fling" of such references before a Puritan Parliament clamps down on the "abuses of players", especially concerning the names of God and Christ. Macbeth himself is, as I have suggested, even pious in his villainy—in company with not a few Shakespearian villains. From the outset he even imagines himself as Lucifer in responding to the choice of Malcolm as Prince of Cumberland (with right of succession to the throne)—just as when at the announcement of the Messiah in the courts of heaven (according to Heb 1:6) that angel refused to obey and was plunged into hell. So Macbeth exclaims, "Stars, hide your fires! / Let not light see my black and deep desires!" (i.4). Subsequently, he imagines himself as Judas on leaving the room of Duncan's last supper, as it were with the parting words of Jesus to Judas ringing in his ears, "That thou doest, do quickly!" (Jn 13:27). So he opens his soliloquy with the reflection, "If 'twere done when 'tis done, then 'twere well / It were done quickly." But then he goes on to reflect on the reasons for not doing the deed, or at least for postponing it—with the pious consideration that Duncan's virtues "Will plead like angels trumpet-tongu'd against / The deep damnation of his taking-off" (i.7). Only, he is soon overborne by his formidable wife.

Again, in Macbeth's approach to the deed of murder, he returns (like Hamlet) to his custom of soliloquizing, with the imagination of a dagger in the air before him—and on its dudgeon he notes "gouts of blood" (ii.1). Where, one wonders, do these "gouts of blood" come from—in the literary sense? Few commentators have noticed their biblical source, in Luke's account of Jesus' agony and sweat of blood in the Garden of Gethsemane, where the Latin Vulgate has *guttae sanguinis* for "drops of blood" (Lk 22:44). Now Macbeth is on his way to murder Duncan, his Christ or anointed king, he fears "the very stones" may "prate of my whereabout"—as it were recalling the hypothetical crying of the stones on Jesus' royal entry into Jerusalem (Lk 19:40). Even after he has done the deed, he remains pious in his horror. He laments his inability to say, "Amen," with Duncan's grooms, though "I had most need of blessing, and 'Amen' / stuck in my throat" (ii.2). Rather, he feels—in common with so many of Shakespeare's characters—like Pilate washing his hands while proclaiming himself innocent of Jesus' blood (Mt 27:24). Then, with a mixture of Pilate and Seneca, he continues, "Will all great Neptune's ocean wash this blood / Clean from my hand? No, this my hand will rather / The multitudinous seas incarnadine, / Making the green one red" (ii.2).

There follows the strange interval of the Porter scene, in which the equally pious, if drunken, Porter imagines himself to be keeper of hell-gate, as in the old mystery play of "The Harrowing of Hell"—while incidentally providing Shakespeare scholars with an important clue for the dating of *Macbeth* in 1606. He speaks of both a "farmer" and an "equivocator", with apparent reference to the Jesuit superior Henry Garnet, whose alias was Farmer and whose defence at his trial in early 1606 involved him in a dispute over the meaning and use of "equivocation". Of more importance to the plot of the play, however, is the Porter's opening of the gate to Macduff, who is from now onwards a key character and who is shortly to become the first witness to the murder of Duncan. This witness of his is given—as it were echoing Macbeth's previous mention of the trumpet tongues of angels—in terms of the Angel of Judgment, as he exclaims before the assembled thanes, "O horror, horror, horror! Tongue nor heart / Cannot conceive nor name thee!" and then, "Confusion now hath made his masterpiece! / Most sacrilegious murder hath broke ope / The Lord's anointed temple, and stole thence / The life o' the building!" (ii.3). His words are commonly understood as implying Shakespeare's own horror at the disclosure of the Gunpowder Plot on November 5, 1605. But the fact is that, unlike Duncan's murder, the plot was never carried out, except in the imaginations of those who pretended to have made the discovery and who inveighed against Father Garnet for his supposed complicity in it.

Now Macduff goes on to summon Banquo, Malcolm, and Donalbain to come and see what he excitedly calls "The great doom's image", to rise as it were from their graves "and walk like sprites / To countenance this horror"—and so he gives the command, "Ring the bell!" (ii.3). The first to come on the scene is Lady Macbeth, who significantly hears the bell as "a hideous trumpet", namely, the angelic trumpet of the last judgment. At the same time, in the world of nature, such strange events have been taking place as "That darkness does the face of earth entomb, / When living light should kiss it" (ii.4)—reminding us not only of the last judgment at the end of the world but also of the hour of Christ's crucifixion, when "from the sixth hour was there darkness over all the land" (Mt 27:45, where Rheims has, "upon the whole earth").

Jumping over the intervening acts, which centre on the murders of Banquo, who knows too much, and Lady Macduff with her children, in revenge for her husband's escape to England, we may come—not for any lack of material, but for its very abundance—to Macbeth's final soliloquy on hearing of his lady's death. This is reported to him by his servant Seyton, whose name, pronounced as "Satan", may suggest a familiar spirit attending on Macbeth like Mephistopheles in Marlowe's *Doctor Faustus*. Here it is noteworthy how rich is this soliloquy in biblical echoes, especially from Psalm 90, where we read, "A thousand years in thy sight are as yesterday when it is past, and as a watch in the night", and "For all our days are passed in thine anger, we have spent our years as a thought", and "We bring our years to an end, as it were a tale that is told." To the words of the Psalm, however, Macbeth adds in his present state of despair, "It is a tale / Told by an idiot, full of sound and fury, / Signifying nothing" (v.5). It is as if he is taking up Lear's initial "Nothing", with its echo of Aristotle, "Nothing will come of nothing", and turning it into his own ending—"full of sound and fury" as he defies his enemies, but in the end all it signifies is "nothing", as though preparatory to another kind of "sound and fury" amid the torments of hell.

Then we come to yet another meta-dramatic dimension, as the dramatist directs our minds from the masterpiece of confusion seen by Macduff in Duncan's murder, not so much to the Gunpowder Plot, when nothing actually happened save (as noted above) in the imaginations of the discoverers, as to that earlier time in the reign of Henry VIII when not one but literally hundreds of temples anointed to the Lord were sacrilegiously broken open and ransacked, in a deed the like of which had never before been known in the history of Christendom. One such deed of despoliation would have been enormity enough, but so many repetitions of the deed to the accompaniment of cruel barbarities inflicted on those who dared to resist the king's command, such as the saintly Richard Whiting, Abbot of Glastonbury, defy one's imagination. From that time onwards it may confidently be said that no historian has begun to realize the depths of evil plumbed by Henry with Thomas Cromwell and his henchmen during those few years from 1536 to 1540. Compared with them all, what was the murder of one king in the dark ages of Scotland, when such murders for ambition's sake were a commonplace, as we may read in chronicles such as those of Holinshed?

Thus once again in the person of Macbeth, as in the persons of Othello and Lear, if for different reasons, we may see the dramatist looking back across the intervening reign of Elizabeth I to that of her father Henry VIII. But now, we may further ask, what of Lady Macbeth? May we not see in her some glimpse of a comparison with Queen Elizabeth—though Henry was her father, while Macbeth was (we may assume) his lady's husband. At least in the strange reason she gives for not having herself done the deed of murdering Duncan, that he "resembled / My father as he slept" (ii.2), commentators have been reminded of Elizabeth's continued reluctance, against the repeated advice of her council, to take the responsibility for having her royal cousin Mary Stuart executed—even after she had signed the death warrant for execution.

At the same time, there is more than a hint at the sufferings of the poor persecuted Catholics of Elizabethan England. There are two notable scenes in which both Lennox with a certain lord in Act III and Malcolm with Macduff in Act IV show themselves on guard against the possibility of the other being an informer. This is what Malcolm himself admits to Macduff in the outcome, "Devilish Macbeth / By many of these trains hath sought to win me / Into his power" (iv.3), and Macbeth admits no less to his lady: "There's not a one of them but in his house / I keep a servant fee'd" (iii.4). Also in the background of Malcolm's long interview with Macduff, both before it begins and after it ends, we are treated to a chorus of lamentation, as in Macduff's complaint, "Each new morn / New widows howl, new orphans cry, new sorrows / Strike heaven on the face", in Malcolm's recognition, "I think our country sinks beneath the yoke, / It weeps, it bleeds, and each new day a gash / Is added to her wounds", and in the subsequent sighs of Ross, "Alas, poor country, / Almost afraid to know itself. It cannot / Be called our mother but our grave . . . / Where sighs and groans and shrieks that rend the air / Are made, not mark'd" (iv.3). That is not Macbeth's Scotland but Shakespeare's England—to whoever knows anything about "the other face" of Elizabethan history.

No Lady in *Timon of Athens*

There is a play of Shakespeare's commonly classed among his "Roman" plays, though the action takes place not in Rome but in Greece, for the simple reason that its plot is largely derived, like the three properly so-called Roman plays, from Plutarch's *Lives of the Greek and Roman Heroes*. Its precise place in Shakespeare's dramatic *oeuvre* is a matter of some uncertainty among scholars, since the text was only printed for the first time in the First Folio of 1623, and it was never performed before then. Rather, the condition of the text as it has come down to us suggests that it was left unfinished— and in this respect it may be considered in connection with *Macbeth*, though in the case of *Macbeth* it seems that the play was somewhat hastily put together for immediate per- formance in the late summer of 1606, whereas *Timon* was simply left unfinished with no performance in view. That is one problem—the practical problem of how and where to deal with a play like Timon in a book like this.

Then there is another problem, similar to that we have had to consider in connection with the other Jacobean plays—or rather, there are three problems. Why did the dramatist choose only one of the Greek heroes from his source in Plutarch? And if he had to choose one, why did he choose such an obscure misanthrope as Timon, when he had a choice among so many more distinguished heroes? And then we may ask, Why, having chosen Timon, did he leave his new play unfinished, as if halfway through he found the hero not sufficiently to his liking? Why didn't he at least foresee, having set his hand to the plough of dramatic composition, that he would have to look back and leave his land unploughed? It is all very mysterious, but on looking more closely at the play, with its plot and characters, we may hope to come upon some convincing explanation.

The plot, to begin with, is somewhat too simple. Timon starts out as a paragon of prodigality. He is too reckless in giving to others, and so when he finds himself reduced to poverty and in need of financial assistance, he comes to realize that his friends have only been (as we say) for fair weather. So he invites them all to a last supper, at which the dishes turn out to be empty and he goes on to vent his indignation on his startled guests. Then, storming out of his house, he takes refuge on the seacoast far from the city of Athens, spending his remaining days as a misanthrope, or hater of mankind. Only in the last scene, after all his fierce railing Lear-like against mankind, he comes to a moment of enlightenment, when, in spite of having been reduced to nothing—though in the process he has come upon a treasure trove of gold—he realizes that "Nothing brings me all things" (v.1).

From the viewpoint of Shakespeare's dramatic art, however, especially as seen in his Jacobean plays, there is one outstanding defect in *Timon of Athens*, which shows it to have been ill conceived from the beginning: its lack of a heroine. Even in two other Roman plays, in *Julius Caesar* (which is so much more of a dramatic success with all its coldly masculine art), there are two minor heroines, Calphurnia and Portia, and in *Coriolanus* (whose art commends itself only to such "classical" critics as T. S. Eliot) we have the hero's mother Volumnia, his wife Virgilia, and the latter's friend Valeria, who are all more or less minor. On the other hand, in *Macbeth* we have a heroine who is no less a villain than the hero, if not more so, as being the efficient cause of his villainy. But in *Timon of Athens* the only women who make so much as an appearance among the *dramatis personae* are the two mistresses of Alcibiades, Phrynia and Timandra, who appear in only one scene, when their only interest is in the gold Timon has discovered.

It is therefore no wonder that Shakespeare, having gone so far in his composition of the play, found that he could go no further. Rather, the wonder is that his fellow actors and editors of the First Folio, John Heminges and Henry Condell, thought fit to publish such an inferior play, while omitting the more genial and successful play of *Pericles*, which shortly followed it.

At least, one may point to indications of a biblical dimension in two significant references to the last supper of Jesus with his disciples—particularly to the moment when Jesus dips a piece of bread into the dish and hands it to Judas (Jn 13:26). Thus early on in the play the cynical philosopher Apemantus remarks, "It grieves me to see so many dip their meat / In one man's blood," adding, "There's much example for't", and " 'T has been prov'd"—as if he (or the dramatist in him) is thinking precisely of the last supper (i.2). Subsequently, there is a nameless stranger who comments, "Why, this is the world's soul, and just of the same piece / Is every flatterer's spirit. Who can call him / His friend that dips in the same dish?" His words are immediately underlined by another stranger with the comment, "Religion groans at it." And then there is yet another who adds, "Men must learn now with pity to dispense, / For policy sits above conscience" (iii.2).

Timon's indignation at the ingratitude of his "friends", which drives him to a state of misanthropy in the second half of the play, shows him as following in the footsteps of Lear, who is likewise driven to madness by indignation at the ingratitude of his false daughters. Implicit, too, in such cases of indignation is the dramatist's own feeling about the betrayal of Jesus by Judas, to which he recurs in so many of his previous Elizabethan plays, both histories (such as *Richard III* and *Richard II*) and comedies (such as *Love's Labour's Lost* and *As You Like It*). Also in more general terms he puts this feeling of his into the mouth of Viola, as heroine in *Twelfth Night*, when she declares, "I hate ingratitude more in a man / Than lying, vainness, babbling drunkenness, / Or any taint of vice whose strong corruption / Inhabits our frail blood" (iii.4).

As for the further dimension of topical religious reference, there is a similar outburst of indignation discernible in Timon's frenzied exclamation, "Put armour on thine ears and on thine eyes, / Whose proof nor yells of mothers, maids, nor babes, / Nor sight of priests in holy vestments bleeding, / Shall pierce a jot" (iv.3). Nothing in the immediate dramatic context seems to indicate anything like what T. S. Eliot has called "an objective correlative" to Timon's emotion, but it may well refer to that other situation indicated in the lamentations of Malcolm, Macduff, and Ross in Macbeth—with this significant difference that, whereas Macduff (for instance) laments how "Each new morn / New widows howl, new orphans cry, new sorrows / Strike heaven on the face" (iv.3), Timon further emphasizes the "sight of priests in holy vestments bleeding", thus pointing unmistakably at the Elizabethan persecution, which was mainly directed against priests and those who might give them shelter. Not that they were actually punished while wearing holy vestments, but not infrequently they were apprehended in the act of saying Mass. This connection is additionally confirmed by the above-quoted remark of the third stranger, that now "Men must learn with pity to dispense, / For policy sits above conscience" (iii.2)—considering that the persecution of Catholics, and particularly of priests, was prompted by motives rather of "policy" than of "conscience".

Such an exclamation, however, as the dramatist dares to put into the mouth of his Timon, even on the excuse of frenzy—which goes beyond even what he had dared to put into the mouth of the mad Lear—may well have made him realize that he had gone too far in a recusant direction, in uttering his true feelings. And it may well have been this reason, more than the others mentioned above, that prompted him to leave the play unfinished, knowing it could hardly be expected to escape the censor's critical attention.

chapter 5
Mistress and Matron

Mistress in *Antony and Cleopatra*

IN THE IMMEDIATE aftermath of the Gunpowder Plot of November 5, 1605, the first performance of *Macbeth* (presumably) in the summer of 1606, and the Act in restraint of abuses of players passed that year, we find Shakespeare dutifully conforming to the requirements of that Act with a series of plays that avoid the danger of a Christian context by dramatizing various stories and characters from Roman history before the coming of Christ. It was as if he was now turning to the task of writing sequels to his earlier Roman play of *Julius Caesar*, while following the same source in Plutarch's *Lives of the Greek and Roman Heroes*, translated into English by Sir Thomas North in 1579. Only the plays he now produced were very different in spirit from *Julius Caesar*, which had first been performed in 1599 for the newly opened Globe Theatre. Of these the first to appear, in 1607, was the tragedy of *Antony and Cleopatra*, which based on events that may make it seem a sequel to the earlier Roman play. But between the two plays there is all the difference that divides the simplicity of republican Rome from the Baroque magnificence not so much of imperial Rome as of Cleopatra's Egypt—not to mention the difference that divides the Elizabethan from the Jacobean age. Moreover, whereas *Julius Caesar* is accorded (as noted above) a cast of mostly male characters, with women represented only by Calphurnia and Portia in minor roles, the hero in the later play is altogether dominated by the feminine, and all but serpentine, character of Cleopatra.

This is what impresses us from the opening scene, in which the art of war, which plays so important a role in *Julius Caesar*, is set aside in favour of the art not so much of peace as of love, in which Cleopatra is a recognized expert. The action in that scene centres on the lingering kiss between the two elderly lovers, with Antony proclaiming, "Let Rome in Tiber melt, and the wide arch / Of the rang'd empire fall! Here is my space" (i.1). In such a kiss, he adds, consists "the nobleness of life". But such grandiose professions of love are undercut by Philo's previous perception of his master as "The triple pillar of the world transform'd / Into a strumpet's fool". Antony himself comes to agree with Philo, when he calls Cleopatra "a triple-turn'd whore" (iv.12), who is "cunning past man's thought" (i.2). So he realizes he must break away from her and return to his duty in Rome, by the side of the other triumvirs, Octavius and Lepidus.

As for Cleopatra's expertise in love, it is fulsomely delineated by Antony's friend Enobarbus in his detailed description of her first meeting with Antony by the river Cydnus, "The barge she sat in, like a burnish'd throne, / Burn'd on the water", while she herself "did lie / In her pavilion— cloth-of-gold tissue— / O'erpicturing that Venus where we see / The fancy outwork nature" (ii.2). In sum, Enobarbus concludes, "Age cannot wither her, nor custom stale / Her infinite variety." Nevertheless, for all the charms of Cleopatra, or rather because of them, Antony feels himself obliged to leave her—as in the remote past Aeneas had to leave

Dido in Carthage—to follow the path of duty directing him to Rome. There he makes his peace with his rival Octavius and receives from him the hand of his chaste sister Octavia in marriage. But the charms of Octavia are soon lost on "the ne'er lust-wearied Antony" (ii.1), and once again we find him longing for the fleshpots of Egypt, and the stronger charms of Cleopatra.

Antony goes straight back to Alexandria. But now he has to face the armed might of his rival Octavius, angered against him owing to his infidelity towards Octavia. And now it is at the promontory of Actium, on the Greek coast, that they are to meet in battle—but whether by sea or land, that is the question. Against the better judgment of his officers, Antony is persuaded by Cleopatra, who promises him sixty ships, to fight his adversary by sea. But then in the midst of the conflict Cleopatra turns back and sails home, and Antony follows her, to the consternation of his friends, one of whom comments, "The greater cantle of the world is lost / With very ignorance. We have kiss'd away / Kingdoms and provinces" (iii.8). When they meet again in Alexandria, they are almost too ashamed to speak to each other. Antony complains, "Thou knew'st too well / My heart was to thy rudder tied by the strings." Yet with a kiss, he adds, "Even this repays me" (iii.9).

A mere kiss, however, cannot solve Antony's practical problem, as the enemy pursues him from Actium to Alexandria. But when he wins a preliminary skirmish, he returns with joy to Cleopatra's embrace, exclaiming, "Leap thou, attire and all, / Through proof of harness to my heart!" and she responds in similar vein, "Lord of lords! / O infinite virtue! Com'st thou smiling from / The world's great snare uncaught?" (iv.8). But again that isn't yet the end. Rather, Octavius's forces are gaining on those of Antony, and what is worse, the latter feels himself betrayed by Cleopatra, whom, for all his love, he cannot trust, and so he turns on her as a "triple-turn'd whore" (iv.10). Then her only expedient is to pretend she is dead, with "Antony!" on her dying lips (iv.11). This news, however, prompts Antony to take his own life, saying, "The long day's task is done, / And we must sleep" (iv.12). He has himself carried to the monument, where he is told the living Cleopatra is awaiting him—and there he dies, to the accompaniment of her lament, "The crown o' the earth doth melt . . . / And there is nothing left remarkable / Beneath the visiting moon" (iv.13).

Before Octavius's victorious forces, and the consequent threat of being taken captive to Rome for his triumphal procession, nothing is now left for Cleopatra but to take her own life—and this she does in dramatic style, like everything else she does. Once again she speaks in high praise of Antony: "His legs bestrid the ocean, his rear'd arm / Crested the world, his voice was propertied / As all the tuned spheres" (v.2). As for herself, now that it comes to taking her own life, she boldly declares, "My resolution's plac'd, and I have nothing / Of woman in me"—in words strangely reminiscent of the unsexed Lady Macbeth. Her plan is to have herself stung to death by an asp, as she herself—in the words of Antony—has something of the "serpent of old Nile" in her (i.5). But first she has a speech to make, for which she needs to put on appropriate attire, "Give me my robe, put on my crown. I have / Immortal longings in me", and so she continues, "I am fire and air, my other elements / I give to baser life" (v.2). Then she says farewell to her attendants, takes the asp, applying it to her breast, and so she, too, dies. Only, what now awaits these suicidal lovers is an Elysium, where, in Antony's expectation, "souls do couch on flowers" (iv.12).

It is all so impressive, with hardly a touch of tragedy. For all the lovers' quarrels with which the love affair of Antony and Cleopatra is interwoven, all leads up to a glorification of adultery and suicide. How different it is from the tragic deaths of father and daughter with which the drama of *King Lear* is brought to a close! It seems as if, in contrast to the metaphysical depth of that play, the dramatist has here chosen to devote, or perhaps even prostitute, his genius to the vast extent of the Roman Empire, with its opposing poles in Rome and Alexandria. The title devised by John Dryden for his revised version of this play, *All for Love* (1677), seems only too appropriate, while raising the question, "What is love in this case of two lovers who have the whole world at their command and are yet prepared to squander it all for the sake of a mutual kiss?" We can't help feeling that Shakespeare has himself been bewitched by "this enchanting queen" (i.2), so as to indulge in the unparalleled recklessness of his lovers—while yet showing both sides of their unrestrained lust, as it were the fruit of that Tree of Knowledge, which combines both good and evil.

The splendour of the play, however, is all on the surface. It allows little room for a meta-dramatic dimension, whether biblical or topical. Occasionally in its vast sweep we come upon echoes of a biblical end of the world—as contrasted with Antony's ideal of Elysium for himself and Cleopatra. Even from the outset we find Antony envisaging their love as fit only for a "new heaven, new earth" (i.1)—in terms of the final vision in both Isaiah (66:22) and the Apocalypse (21:1). And at the end, in the exchange of the two guards, "The star is fallen" / "And time is at his period" (iv.12), we may recognize another echo of the Apocalypse, where mention is made of a star that falls from heaven to earth (9:1)—recalling the similar exchange in *King Lear* between Kent and Edgar: "Is

this the promis'd end?" / "Or image of that horror?" (v.3).
Even in the mouth of Cleopatra there is mention of "dooms-
day" (v.2). From the lips of Antony himself come two
unconscious parodies of the account of Christ's passion, both
from John's Gospel, "For one death / Might have prevented
many" (iv.10, cf. Jn 11:50), and "The time is come" (iv.12,
cf. John 17:1). After all, when it comes to tragedy, for all its
apparent splendour, Shakespeare cannot rid his mind of biblical, and especially apocalyptic, references.

On the other hand, what he evidently has on his mind in
his characterization of Cleopatra, in her relation to Antony,
is not so much biblical as topical. For here we may well find
Shakespeare's long considered response to the challenge
offered him, under the name of "Melicert", by Henry Chettle in *England's Mourning Garment* (1603). Chettle was
complaining of Shakespeare's silence when England's other
poets were all in mourning for the death of their great
queen. No doubt, Shakespeare had reasons of his own for
refusing—in sympathy with other recusants—to join in that
chorus. But a delayed response has been seen in his characterization of Cleopatra, in whom (as noted above), as also in
the former queen, good and evil are inextricably intermin-
gled. As for Antony, his prototype is likewise seen in the
Earl of Essex, as being the last and most regretted of the old
queen's amours. He both loved her and rebelled against her,
and in view of his rebellion she signed a reluctant death warrant—as she had previously signed the death warrant for
Mary Queen of Scots. And these two regrets she carried
with her to her troubled deathbed.

Matron in *Coriolanus*

So far from following up his *Antony and Cleopatra* with a
sequel on Augustan Rome, Shakespeare preferred to look

back in the history of Rome to a more primitive age when
the city was but one of many warring city-states in the region
of Latium. Maybe in that early age he longed to obtain a
breath of fresh air, away from the perfumes and enchantments, the luxuries and cruelties, of Cleopatra's Egypt. So we
find in this new play of *Coriolanus* a notable change from the
vastness and splendour of the former play, with its continual
movement among so many scenes between Rome and
Alexandria, taking in the whole extent of the Mediterranean
Sea, to the narrow limits of pristine Rome, as seen through
the self-regarding eyes of one heroic individual. Here the
dramatist may have achieved, at least according to the refined
taste of T. S. Eliot, something approaching the classical ideal
of dramatic art, but he evidently failed to snatch anything
that might be called "a grace", according to the other taste of
Alexander Pope, "beyond the reach of art".

For one thing, the hero is cursed, whether by the historian or the dramatist, with a singularly unlovable character.
He is too wrapped up in his own self-importance and pride
in his deeds of valour to be welcomed even by those of his
own side, the lordly patricians of Rome, let alone by his
opponents, the tribunes of Rome with the people behind
them. He may have won the war against the Volscians on
behalf of Rome, with his own strong arm, but he is consti-
tutionally (in both senses of the word) incapable of winning
the peace, for which he has to condescend to sue the people
for their votes, as a candidate (wearing the *toga candida*, or
white robe). He is too easily angered at the people, and too
readily baited by the envious tribunes. So in his indignation,
like Lear in the storm, he goes forth from the city and
throws in his lot with his Volscian enemies, whom he now
leads against Rome. Not all the pleading of his patrician
friends is of any avail, till his formidable mother Volumnia,

from whose breast he has sucked his valour even from infancy, pleads with him for the city. Then at last he feels his heart melting and he realizes he is not "Of stronger earth than others" (v.3). He yields to her pleas, but with the reluctant protest, "O mother, mother, / What have you done? Behold, the heavens do ope, / The gods look down, and this unnatural scene / They laugh at." His words are impressive, the most impressive words he utters in the whole course of the play, but they are pointless. Now he cannot return to Rome. All he can do is to go back to his enemies, who take little time to contrive his murder. And that is all.

The plot of *Coriolanus* is thus for Shakespeare, who usually thrives on complication, a comparatively simple one—varied only by the furious outbursts of the hero against his enemies, in which he may bear comparison with Lear and Timon. Insofar as the play is to be seen as artistic, in the opinion of T. S. Eliot, it is a cold, classical art, if heated up at times with the hero's anger. It is also varied by the arguments of his friends, as they try to persuade him to swallow his pride and humble himself, in order to obtain the necessary votes of the people, and then by the taunts of his enemies, the tribunes, whose vituperation he is unable to stand for long. But—and this is a big "but"—the play is unredeemed by any feminine grace. Here is no Desdemona, no Cordelia, to qualify the folly of an Othello, or a Lear, but only the stern mother Volumnia, who in other circumstances might (we imagine) have been a Goneril or a Lady Macbeth. There is also a wife, Virgilia, with her friend Valeria. But these women have even more minor roles to play in this one-man performance of *Coriolanus* than either Calphurnia or Portia in *Julius Caesar*.

Only the final appeal of Volumnia, with which she persuades her dragonish son to give up his revenge against

Rome, serves to prompt his impressive response, "O mother, mother, / What have you done?"—and that in turn may recall the other impressive words of Isabella to Angelo in *Measure for Measure*, "But man, proud man . . . , / Plays such fantastic tricks before high heaven / As make the angels weep, who with our spleens / Would all themselves laugh mortal" (ii.2). His protest, however, like Isabella's appeal, is pointless, for all its poetry. His mother cannot retract what she has said, nor can he in his pride return to Rome. He can only await the certain descent of doom as he rejoins the Volscians, while in her, even in her appeal to her son, there is no redeeming grace. She herself is but a dragon, and it is she who has reared him up to be another such dragon.

Consequently, for all Eliot's admiration of Shakespeare's dramatic art in *Coriolanus*, there is no such *catharsis* or purification of emotion as is essential to the art of drama. Nor, as Milton says in his own drama of *Samson Agonistes*, is there anything for tears. All, as in *Antony and Cleopatra*, is on the surface of drama, with the result that neither play can truly be termed a "tragedy"—save insofar as the hero dies at the end, just as in the earlier play both hero and heroine take their own lives. For none of them can we feel the deep pity we do for Othello and Desdemona, Lear and Cordelia. Nor, so far as I can see, is there much of a biblical dimension, apart from a solitary mention of "th' end o' the world" with reference to the hero (iii.1)—which merely serves to show how close is the idea of tragedy in Shakespeare's mind to the other idea of eschatology. Nor can I see much of a topical dimension in the play either, save insofar as the dramatist may have been thinking of his own mother, Mary Arden, (who died at this time, in 1608) in the person of Volumnia—but that is mere speculation. All in all, with all respect to T. S. Eliot, *Coriolanus* has to be judged a dramatic failure, even as a work of art—a judgment that has been amply vindicated by the lack of performances both in the dramatist's own lifetime and thereafter. Nor was it even granted the doubtful honour in the Restoration of being rewritten—like *Antony and Cleopatra* in the form of Dryden's *All For Love*—in a revised version. Thus people have voted with their feet, whether against the hero of this play or against his dramatist. It is, like *Timon of Athens*, another instance of Shakespeare's nodding acquaintance with Homer. ■

chapter 6

Two Romantic Heroines

▨ Marina in *Pericles*

THERE IS, FIRST, a strange gap in Shakespeare's dramatic inspiration following on the exposure of the Gunpowder Plot in 1605 with the trials of the plotters in 1606—a gap filled in not only by *Macbeth*, as the last of his "Christian" plays, but also by his three "Roman" plays. Then we come upon an equally strange revival of that inspiration in a play that Shakespeare's friend and rival Ben Jonson contemptuously dismissed as "the mouldy tale" of *Pericles*. It is as if, for all the seeming splendour of *Antony and Cleopatra*, as opposed to the gloomy poetic speeches of *Macbeth*, Shakespeare has once again returned to the true source of his dramatic inspiration in the person of an ideal heroine, once again described in terms reminiscent of mediaeval devotion to the Virgin Mary as "full of grace". Before, in his first two Jacobean tragedies we have noticed such heroines as Desdemona and Cordelia, and in his two "problematic" comedies such other heroines as Isabella and Helena. But Lady Macbeth is no such heroine! Nor is Cleopatra, for all her Egyptian enchantments! Nor is the dragonish Volumnia! Only now, over the darkened mind of the dramatist there dawns as it were another sign of the "woman clothed with the sun"

(Rev 12:1), in the heroine of *Pericles*, Marina—who not only is "born at sea", as her name indicates, but in whom both her father and the dramatist himself are "born again".

Once again, therefore, the question arises, What was it that put it into Shakespeare's mind to take up the subject of "Pericles"—or rather the old story of "Apollonius of Tyre" as told in the late fourteenth century by Chaucer's contemporary, John Gower, in his *Confessio Amantis*? And then there is the further question, Why was it that this play, which Shakespeare brought to such a successful completion with such a splendid awakening of his dramatic genius, should have been omitted from the First Folio by his fellow actors and co-editors, and only included in a second issue of the Third Folio of 1663, which appeared the following year? It is all very strange—yet all of a piece with the dramatist himself and his writings.

These questions may be answered, in part, by the evident fact that the play isn't entirely or originally Shakespeare's. Apparently, it was first taken in hand by a younger colleague in the King's Men, a recusant named George Wilkins, who began the play but left it unfinished, while going on to write a prose version of the story, in which the name of Apollonius is already changed into Pericles. (That change of name must have been necessitated by the metrical requirements of blank verse, which are met by "Pericles" but not by "Apollonius"—though the precise choice of "Pericles" remains a question.) But still we have to ask, Why did Wilkins leave his play unfinished, and continue with his prose version instead? And then, Why did Shakespeare choose to take up the play from where Wilkins had left off, apparently from the beginning of Act III? Did Shakespeare notice something in those first two acts that may have led him to offer his services for the remaining acts—as if he had found something in them that specially appealed to him?

One interesting hypothesis is that in what Wilkins had already written, especially in Act I, Shakespeare may have noticed a strange similarity between the story of King Antiochus with his daughter and a scandalous rumour spread among Catholic exiles and others on the European continent concerning Henry VIII with Anne Boleyn—to the effect that Anne was not only Henry's second wife but also his daughter by her mother Elizabeth Boleyn. This rumour is recorded by the eminent Catholic exiled theologian Nicholas Sander, in his Latin work *De Origine ac Progressu Schismatis Anglicani*, which wasn't published till after his death in 1585, and in various translations, but not in English till the mid-nineteenth century, when it was translated by David Lewis as *The Rise and Growth of the Anglican Schism* (1877). No doubt it was because of the highly scandalous nature of this rumour that the book remained untranslated into English for so long, and the rumour itself has largely been ignored by historians as beneath their attention. More recently, however, it has been partly vindicated, partly refuted by Peter Butcher in a book entitled *Where Credit is Due* (1994), in which he convincingly proves that Anne Boleyn was the daughter not of Henry VIII but of her uncle Thomas Howard, Duke of Norfolk, as the fruit of a no less scandalous affair he had with his own sister, Elizabeth Howard Boleyn. Is it possible that Archbishop Cranmer, when declaring that Henry's marriage with Anne had been null and void from the outset, had been informed of this disgraceful fact, possibly by the king himself?

For Shakespeare to have taken up this subject from the recusant pen of George Wilkins, in an age when spectators and readers were on the alert for the discovery of hidden meanings (more than scholars are prepared to admit today), might well have been a perilous undertaking. Still, he was protected by his position in the King's Men and by the fact that he didn't dramatize the story till well on into the reign of James I. It may also have been for this reason that he went out of his way to emphasize the mouldiness of the tale by inserting the Chorus of "ancient Gower" in the beginning of each act and in the end of the play, if only for the sake of disguising its dangerous topicality. Then out of this scandalous situation between King Antiochus and his unnamed daughter (and wife) Shakespeare takes over and develops the story as a moral play of good being drawn out of evil. So while King Antiochus and his daughter may be seen as corresponding to King Henry and Anne Boleyn, Pericles himself need have no special topical correspondence beyond that of representing the old Catholic faith in England, pursued by the unrelenting anger first of Henry, then of Elizabeth, owing to this knowledge of the damning truth concerning them.

What is of central importance to Shakespeare, however, in his decision to develop the story as left by George Wilkins, is not so much the scandal, which is but his starting point, as the further marriage of Pericles with Thaisa in Act II and the subsequent birth of Marina in Act III, along with Thaisa's apparent death in giving birth and her burial at sea. Then, because of the unrelenting persecution of Antiochus, Pericles is obliged to leave his newborn baby with Cleon, governor of Tarsus, and his wife Dionyza. But then, as Marina grows to maidenhood, Dionyza grows jealous of her beauty, which she fears may distract the attention of possible suitors for her own daughter. So she entrusts her servant Leonine with the task of secretly putting Marina to death. In the nick of time, however, Marina is saved by pirates, only to be sold into prostitution at Mitylene—where she defies all clients with her insistent profession of chastity.

It is at this juncture that the weary Pericles is brought by ship to the harbour of Mitylene, and Marina is brought on board to entertain him with her singing. It is also at this juncture that the sleeping genius of Shakespeare is at last awakened to the prospect of another recognition scene, such as he had produced for the poor old Lear with the coming of Cordelia in Act IV. Then, however, the blissful joy of Lear had been overtaken by an agony of sorrow over the death of his innocent daughter, and so (it may be conjectured) the genius of the dramatist had fallen into a long stupor, from which he only now recovers on the similar occasion of this other reunion between Pericles and Marina. In other words, in the character of Pericles we may now see a reflection of no other than Shakespeare himself.

At first, the aged hero is filled with admiration at the sight of this young girl, whom he sees (in Viola's similar words in *Twelfth Night* ii.4) "Like Patience gazing on kings' graves, and smiling / Extremity out of act" (v.1). Then, on learning that her name is Marina, or born at sea, he makes inquiries into her origin and parentage, and with each answer his amazement increases, till he realizes that she is indeed his long-lost daughter. Such is his joy that, like Lear pricking himself with a pin, he asks to be put to present pain, "Lest this great sea of joys rushing upon me / O'erbear the shores of my mortality, / And drown me with their sweetness." Then, addressing Marina, he calls her "Thou that begett'st him that did thee beget"—recalling the words addressed by St. Bernard to the Virgin Mary in Dante's *Paradiso* cxxxiii, *"Vergine Madre, Figlia del tuo Figlio"*, which Chaucer renders in his Second Nun's Prologue to the *Canterbury Tales* as "Thou maid and mother, daughter of thy Son". Or he may be recalling the earlier words of the liturgical hymn, *Ave Redemptoris Mater, "Tu quae genuisti, / Natura mirante, tuum sanctum Genitorem"*—Thou who gavest birth, amid the wonder of Nature, to the holy one who gave birth to thee.

Now amid his newfound bliss on this discovery of his daughter, Pericles imagines he hears the music of the spheres—recalling the liturgy of angels described by Lorenzo to Jessica in the happy ending of *The Merchant of Venice*—and in his slumber he receives a vision of the goddess Diana instructing him to repair to her temple at Ephesus. There, under Diana's sacred auspices, he is further reunited with his long-lost wife Thaisa, now restored to him in a strange miracle of healing, thanks to the medical art of the Ephesian physician Caerimon. For the dramatist, too, it is a renewal of the similar restoration of the abbess Aemilia to her long-lost husband Aegeon, also at Ephesus, in the climax of *The Comedy of Errors*. Here the pagan setting of Ephesus, with its worship of Diana as Earth-Mother and goddess of chastity, may be interpreted as Shakespeare's way of getting round the Puritan Act in restraint of players, by availing himself of the correspondences worked out in the Florentine Platonism of Ficino and Pico della Mirandola between the "deities" of paganism and Christianity—as between Jupiter and God the Father (in *Cymbeline*), Apollo and Christ the Son (in *The Winter's Tale*), and here Diana and Mary as Virgin and Mother.

Moreover, everything in this play from the time it was taken over by Shakespeare points from Marina, as "born at sea", to Mary, who was hailed by St. Bernard (mistaking the derivation of the name from the Latin *mare*, or "sea") as *Stella Maris*. Again, it points from the goddess Diana, with her temple at Ephesus, to the Virgin Mary, whose title "Mother of God" (*Theotokos* in Greek) was first officially proclaimed at the Council of Ephesus in A.D. 431. So in her we may recognize the inspiration, or divine muse, that enabled the dramatist to jump over the years of "penury"— in the Scottish play and the "Roman" plays—from the former years of "plenty", with Desdemona and Cordelia, Isabella and Helena, to the latter years, with Marina and Perdita, Imogen and Miranda, culminating in Katharine. In other words, it is to the Virgin Mary that we have to attribute the whole inspiration of the Jacobean Shakespeare.

Perdita in *The Winter's Tale*

If one takes the "final romances" of Shakespeare in the order of chronological composition, one would have to deal with Imogen in *Cymbeline* before coming to Perdita with Hermione in *The Winter's Tale*. All the same, there is a certain fitness in taking *Pericles* with *The Winter's Tale*, considering the remarkable parallelism of their plots—as if the dramatist is setting out to fulfil in the latter play what he only half accomplished in the former, on the basis of work taken in hand from another. Then, comparing the two plays, whereas the background to the former covers almost the whole seaboard of the eastern Mediterranean, the latter is more simply limited to the contrasting countries of Sicilia and Bohemia. All Shakespeare seems to have done is to take the old pastoral romance of Robert Greene, *Pandosto* (1588), and made it into a play—as if in ironical revenge for Greene's old criticism of him in his *Groatsworth of Wit* (1592) as "an upstart crow, beautified with our feathers".

What is more, the story he found in *Pandosto*, the hero's recovery of both a long-lost daughter and a long-lost wife, would have struck the dramatist as almost a duplication of what he had already dramatized in *Pericles*—which is a main reason for taking the two plays together. There is also a perfect match between these plays in the manner of their happy ending, only they differ from each other in that the losses suffered by Pericles at sea are due not to any fault of his own but to an unkind Fate, whereas the hero of *The Winter's*

Tale, Leontes King of Sicilia, is entirely responsible for the losses both of his wife Hermione and of his daughter Perdita. In this respect, his folly is comparable to that of Lear, in whose name one may notice a parallel to his own, with the royal meaning of "lion".

Then there is a significant difference between the romance as told by Greene and the play as presented by Shakespeare. For in the play the two countries of Sicilia and Bohemia are simply switched from the romance, in such a way as to provide Bohemia with a seacoast it never had in European history—and to provide Ben Jonson with another of his snide remarks at Shakespeare's expense (as in the case of *Pericles*). For Greene, as a classical scholar, Sicily was the island of shepherds and pastoral romance, as idealized in the *Idylls* of Theocritus, whereas Shakespeare places his pastoral and rural scenery in Bohemia, while concentrating on Sicilia for the main tragi-comic action of his play. Why this seemingly unnecessary change? Simply, I suggest, that the dramatist has in mind not the classical land of Sicilia (known in those times as Trinacria, or three-cornered island) but his own land of England (which also has three corners, West from Dungeness to Land's End, and North to Berwick-on-Tweed).

I would carry this suggestion even further, in view of the topological dimension of the play, and see in Leontes' Sicilia a replica of Henry's England. This dimension I find already apparent in the second scene, featuring the state visit of Polixenes, King of Bohemia, to Leontes, his brother of Sicilia, and as it were anticipating the similar opening of *Henry VIII* with the formal and expensive meeting of the English and French kings at the Field of the Cloth of Gold. Leontes, with his name (like that of Lear) recalling the heraldic lion, may also echo the saying of Sir Thomas More in warning Cromwell against letting the lion (namely the king) know his own strength. Then, if Leontes is Henry, who is Hermione but Henry's first lawful wife, Katharine of Aragon? And then, just as Leontes conceives a sudden, unexplained jealousy against Hermione, accusing her of adultery with Polixenes, so Henry is not so much jealous of Katharine as conscience-stricken (as he claims) about the validity of their marriage, or rather the original dispensation of the Pope. Their two situations lead up to a trial in which the queen, in either case a foreigner, but daughter to a great monarch (Hermione to the emperor of Russia, Katharine to the king of Spain), makes her appeal to a religious authority beyond the sea—Hermione to the oracle of Apollo at Delphos, Katharine to the Pope of Rome. And in either case their appeal is upheld.

Such is the dramatic context within which Perdita, whose name means "the lost one", or rather "the lost grace" *(perdita gratia)* of her father Leontes, is born to Hermione in prison. When the baby is brought by Paulina, wife of the courtier Antigonus, to its father, Leontes refuses to recognize it as his child, affirming that it is obviously the fruit of the adultery between Hermione and Polixenes—in spite of Paulina's insistence on its resemblance to him. He therefore orders Antigonus to take the baby and expose it on some remote shore. There on the coast of Bohemia, while Antigonus is devoured by a bear, the little Perdita is found by a shepherd and brought up as his daughter. Then, after the lapse of some sixteen years explained by the Chorus Time, the son of Polixenes, Prince Florizel, comes courting the lovely shepherdess Perdita, attired as queen on the occasion of a sheep-shearing feast in the rural countryside. Polixenes himself is also present in disguise, suspecting the romantic intentions of the prince, and when he has assured himself that his suspicions are true, he reveals himself and charges his son with bestowing his favours on an unworthy country girl. On his angry departure, the couple decide to make their escape by ship to Sicilia, and there a double reunion takes place (as in the happy ending of *Pericles*) first between father and daughter, Leontes and Perdita, and then between husband and wife. For now it transpires that Hermione never died but after she had swooned at her trial she was kept in confinement by the faithful Paulina till the time should come for such a reunion. Thus Shakespeare more than fulfils the promise both of Act IV in *King Lear* and of Act V in *Pericles*, in yet another dramatic rendering of Christ's parable of the prodigal son implied in the name of Perdita as Leontes' "lost grace".

There remain two other major characters in the play who call for our attention. One is Polixenes, who is hardly to be identified with the amorous King Francis I of France, for all his meeting with King Henry VIII at the Field of the Cloth of Gold. He might well have been an object of suspicion to Henry in a question of adultery—save that Katharine of Aragon prudently stayed at home in England, while the two kings were celebrating their short-lived treaty of alliance in France. On the other hand, the name "Polixenes", from its Greek meaning of "many guests", may tell us something of his identity, as one who offers hospitality to many visitors from abroad. Subsequently, a more precise identification is suggested by the words with which Leontes welcomes Florizel to his Sicilian court, and adds concerning his royal father, "You have a holy father, / A graceful gentleman, against whose person, / So sacred as it is, I have done sin" (v.1). These are strange words, when understood in a naturalistic sense, but when we take into account the topological allegory that runs through the play with reference to Henry VIII and Katharine, they point to one individual, the sacred person of the holy father, the Pope in Rome, against whom Henry has most certainly "done sin"—both in his wilful separation from Rome for the sake of obtaining his divorce from Katharine and in his ruthless spoliation of the monasteries.

The other character is the trusted adviser to Leontes, Camillo, whom the king has trusted "With all the things nearest to my heart, as well / My chamber-councils, wherein, priest-like, thou / Hast cleans'd my bosom" (i.2). On finding himself requested by the king in his frenzy to poison Polixenes in revenge, Camillo cannot bring himself to do so, but instead he warns Polixenes of his peril and helps him to escape. He himself accompanies Polixenes back to Bohemia, and subsequently to the sheep-shearing feast, where he remains behind after the king has left in anger. It is he who now assists the dejected couple to find a ship to carry them to Sicilia, while on another ship he follows in company with Polixenes. Thus it is he who, no less than Paulina, helps to bring the former tragedy to its tragi-comic conclusion. Then in terms of the England of Henry VIII, who, it may be asked, may correspond to such a faithful counsellor if not Sir Thomas More? He it was who sided with Katharine and her reliance on the Pope, for which he incurred the displeasure of both the king and his new queen, Anne Boleyn, in consequence of which he lost his head on Tower Hill in 1535 as a "traitor". This identification we may also recognize in other such figures of a faithful counsellor in the last plays, Helicanus in *Pericles*, Belarius in *Cymbeline*, and especially Gonzalo in *The Tempest*—though in the final history play of *Henry VIII* he is merely mentioned in words of praise, without making an actual appearance.

Now to return to Perdita, from her first emergence in Bohemia as a maiden in the second half of the play, she is introduced to us by the Chorus Time as "now grown in grace / Equal with wondering". Now we see her as indeed, like Cordelia in *King Lear*, a personification of the "lost grace", or *gratia perdita*, of her father Leontes, who is the prodigal son in this play no less than Lear in his. At the sheep-shearing feast she is indeed, not merely in outward show "Most goddess-like prank'd up", but in truth such that, as Florizel exclaims, "all your acts are queens". Polixenes himself recognizes that "nothing she does or seems / But smacks of something greater than herself, / Too noble for this place" (iv.3). This recognition of her grace makes his sudden outburst of anger against her and his son no less irrational (as it is intended to appear) than the earlier outburst of Leontes against Hermione.

This anger of Polixenes, however, has the providential effect of driving the unhappy lovers to Sicilia, for the ideal reunion between Leontes and Perdita and the recovery of his lost grace—as subsequently for the reunion between him and his long-lost wife Hermione. Then, amid all these reunions the keyword is "grace", as when Leontes addresses Florizel and Perdita on their arrival in Sicilia (but before he has come to recognize her as his daughter) as "You gracious couple", while remembering Florizel's father as "A graceful gentleman". When Polixenes and Camillo arrive in pursuit of the couple, all is duly explained and misunderstandings are cleared up, and then, we hear, "a notable passion of wonder appeared in them", and "such a deal of wonder is broken out within this hour" that, it seems, "every wink of an eye some new grace will be born" (v.2). It is indeed a cumulation of grace. Yet more remains, when Paulina leads them to the supposed "statue" of Hermione, which turns out to be Hermione herself in a "miracle" of resurrection such as we have already seen in the case of Thaisa at the end of *Pericles*—or, one may add, in the case of Hero in *Much Ado*

About Nothing. Finally, the theme of "grace" is brought to its completion in the concluding prayer of Hermione for her newly found daughter Perdita, "You gods, look down, / And from your sacred vials pour your graces / Upon my daughter's head!"

chapter 7
Two British Heroines

■ Imogen in *Cymbeline*

ONCE AGAIN, not least in approaching such an inferior
play (by Shakespearian standards) as *Cymbeline*, we find
ourselves facing the question, What was it in the story that
led the dramatist to choose it as the subject of one of his last
romances? At least, he may have found in it some parallel
with the story of *King Lear*, as a British play with its main
outlines taken from Shakespeare's favourite source, Holinshed's *Chronicles*—though some seven centuries divided the
age of Lear from that of Cymbeline, who lived (as Holinshed notes) at the time of Christ's nativity. Another notable
difference is not only in time but also in place, for whereas
in *King Lear* the dramatist made not a single mention of
"Britain" in the whole course of the play—but only of
"British" forces ranged against Lear and Cordelia in the last
battle—in *Cymbeline* he repeats the name of that country
more than twenty times. This may be, as suggested above in
dealing with *King Lear*, that in the former play Shakespeare
was aiming at a greater universality, looking beyond the limits of place and time, whereas in the latter play he has in
mind the Britain (including England and Wales) not only of
Cymbeline but also (in a topical allegory) of Henry VIII.

Already from the beginning we may notice this topical implication in the situation of the court, with the opening words of a Gentleman, "You do not meet a man but frowns." All this frowning is occasioned by the misfortune of the Princess Imogen, who has just married a gentleman named Posthumus Leonatus, and so, like Desdemona at the beginning of *Othello*, she has incurred her father's anger, since he has intended her for the worthless son of his second wife. So she is now to be imprisoned, while her husband is to be banished, but the frowning is because of the sympathy in which the two are held, in contrast to the disfavour with which the new queen and her son are popularly regarded. Cymbeline himself now enters and, after venting his anger on the lingering Posthumus, as "Thou basest thing!" he directs the same rage against his daughter, calling her "disloyal thing", "past grace", "thou vile one", and "Thou foolish thing". He is altogether too free with "things"!

As for the precise topicality of this situation, if Cymbeline anticipates Henry VIII, who preferred to think of himself, being a Welsh Tudor, as King of Britain, his new queen would be Anne Boleyn, who never won the popularity enjoyed among the English people by Katharine of Aragon. And then Imogen would stand for Henry's daughter by Katharine, the Princess Mary—though Anne never had a son for her to marry. Only here we find no mention of Imogen's mother, the first queen of Cymbeline. She has to remain without a name, like the first wife of King Lear, Cordelia's mother, and like the exiled duke in *As You Like It*.

Following Posthumus Leonatus to his land of exile in Rome, we find ourselves in the midst of another plot of jealousy, derived from a story in Boccaccio's *Decameron*. This is a wager plot, in which Posthumus rashly boasts and even bets on the fidelity of his wife Imogen, and his bet is taken up by a friend, who now proves to be the villain of this minor plot, Iachimo (as it were a little Iago). In pursuit of the bet, Iachimo makes his way to Britain, ostensibly to bring Imogen news of her husband, but really to tempt her virtue, or at least to make it seem as if she has yielded to his importunity. Meanwhile, in Rome, according to Iachimo's glowing description of him to Imogen, Posthumus has achieved such eminence that "He sits 'mongst men like a descended god. / He hath a kind of honour sets him off, / More than a mortal seeming." He further compliments her on "the election of a sir so rare, / Which you know cannot err" (i.6). These are strange words to be applied to a mere exile in Rome, but if we recall those other strange words addressed by Leontes to Florizel about his father Polixenes, the barely disguised topical reference can be to none other than the Pope. For the Pope has to achieve his position as supreme pontiff through the "election" of the college of cardinals, and he also claims the charism of infallibility when proclaiming a dogma on faith or morals to be held by the universal Church. No wonder that Imogen, in maintaining her loyalty to Posthumus, like the Princess Mary in remaining loyal to the Pope, has incurred the fierce anger of her Henry-like father! But then Cymbeline is under the influence of his new queen, who is also responsible (as we learn at the end of the play) for the discontinuance of his customary tribute to Rome.

In the development of this secondary plot of jealousy— which may remind us in many ways of *Othello*, not only for its theme but also the name of the villain—Iachimo, having wormed his way into favour with Imogen by his praise of her husband, manages by a trick to remain in her room after she has retired to bed. Then, while she is sleeping, he notes certain private marks on her body which he may describe to Posthumus back in Rome as evidence of her infidelity.

Then, having returned to Rome, he presents Posthumus with his "refutation" of the latter's boasting. The husband's anger, like that of Othello against Desdemona, knows no bounds. Not only does he despair, like Hamlet, of all women, seeing that Imogen is so faithless, but he even plans to have her poisoned in the approved Italian fashion. He also finds means of returning to Britain in the Roman army, now about to be sent there under the command of Lucius for enforcing the interrupted payment of tribute to Rome.

Meanwhile, back in Britain Imogen has learnt of Posthumus's jealousy and is no less troubled about it than Desdemona was on realizing that Othello was jealous of her. But when urged by Iachimo to take revenge on her husband, she is too bewildered even to entertain the thought. "Reveng'd!" she repeats in amazement, "How should I be reveng'd?" (i.6). Then Iachimo has to take back what he has said, pleading that it was but to test her. Subsequently, she has to deal with the unwelcome attentions of the queen's unworthy son Cloten, who comes to her chamber in the early morning to rouse her with the song, "Hark, hark! The lark at heaven's gate sings" (ii.2)—recalling the song of the unfaithful Proteus sung in honour of Silvia in *Two Gentlemen of Verona*, "Who is Silvia?" (iv.2) Then, just as Silvia flees from Milan to join her true lover Valentine in the forest, so Imogen escapes from her father's court and makes her way to Wales in male disguise, in the hope of meeting her husband in the army of Lucius on their landing at Milford Haven.

Here in the wilds of Wales she meets the old counsellor Belarius who, like Camillo fleeing from the anger of Leontes, has had to flee from the other anger of Cymbeline on account of his loyalty to Rome. With him he brought the two infant sons of the king and brought them up far from the perils of "the envious court" (*As You Like It* ii.1). They all welcome her as a handsome young man and even regard her, even in her male disguise, as "an angel", "an earthly paragon", and "divine" (iii.6)—words reserved by Shakespeare for the ideal heroines in his Jacobean plays. While they are away and she is resting in their cave, she takes the medicine prepared for her (made at the request of the wicked queen to poison her, but altered by the court doctor so as to have an effect similar to that prepared for Juliet by Friar Laurence), and she falls into a slumber that looks like death. While she is in this condition, the young princes find her and think she is really dead. So they conduct a simple funeral service for her, with the well-known dirge, "Fear no more the heat of the sun."

Anyhow, to simplify a long and complicated story—surely one of the most complicated and incredible in all Shakespearian drama, including some twenty-four knots to be unravelled in the final scene—its whole movement is directed, like that of *King Lear* to Dover, to one place, the harbour of Milford Haven, whither come both the invading force of Romans under Lucius and the repelling British army under Cymbeline. (It was also at Milford Haven that Henry Richmond arrived in Wales, before going on to engage Richard III in battle at Bosworth.) In the battle that now takes place, the Romans seem to be gaining over the British, till the tide of conflict is turned by the two young British princes with the old Belarius. Before the battle, however, Posthumus, who is with the Romans, has a vision in which the god Jupiter descends on his eagle, bearing a message with a prophetic, but enigmatic, meaning, about "a lion's whelp" (meaning Leonatus, as "born of a lion") and "a piece of tender air" (referring to the Latin for "woman", *mulier,* interpreted as *mollis aer,* or "tender air"), also about "a stately cedar" from whose branches a new tree will grow (as it were prophesying the offspring to come from his union with Imogen).

Then in the final scene it is first announced that "the queen is dead"—in simple words that seem to echo the news brought by Seyton of the similar end of Lady Macbeth (v.5)—"with horror, madly dying", who "being cruel to the world, concluded / Most cruel to herself". Then Posthumus with Belarius and the two princes appear before Cymbeline, as well as Imogen, and there takes place a general reunion and reconciliation, bringing such joy to the old king—as in the previous plays of *King Lear* (iv.7) and *Pericles* (v.1)—that he exclaims, on learning that it is his daughter Imogen who is before him, "If this be so, the gods do mean to strike me / To death with mortal joy!" He also adds, as though in the spirit of Cordelia (whose tears are also compared to "holy water", iv.3), "My tears that fall / Prove holy water on thee!" He then promises Lucius that, though the British have defeated the Romans in battle, he will "submit to Caesar, / And to the Roman Empire", proclaiming a harmonious peace in which "A Roman and a British ensign" shall "wave / Friendly together" (v.5).

The topical relevance of this conclusion is too obvious to need comment—combining the dramatist's wishful thinking concerning the old reign of Henry VIII with the present, pacific ideals of James I, in relation to Christian Rome. It is a sign that in Shakespeare's mind the sadness attending the tragic outcome of *King Lear*, in view of the real situation of English Catholics, has given place in his final tragi-comedies to a romantic dream of what might have happened IF only Henry VIII had (like Cymbeline and Leontes) repented of his sins against Rome before the end of his earthly life.

Katharine in *Henry VIII*

From *Cymbeline*, which is commonly dated about 1609, several years were to pass before the first performance of

Henry VIII on June 29, 1613. And that was long after Shakespeare had bid farewell to the stage with his Epilogue to *The Tempest* in 1611. Yet it is not inappropriate to make such a jump in order to emphasize the important place of *Henry VIII* in the Jacobean drama of Shakespeare, seeing that almost everything from *Othello* and *King Lear* seems to lead up to it. It is almost as if the dramatist had foreseen, and planned, such a succession of plays from the beginning. In this succession everything seems to fit into a providential order, which Shakespeare is obeying without perhaps fully realizing what he is doing, but responding to some direction in his subconscious mind. Only, once he reaches the climax and proceeds to dramatize the reign itself, the great Shakespeare seems to falter, and, as before in the case of *Henry V*, he finds himself unequal to the great task he has set himself.

Or, we may ask, is that really the case? In *Henry V* the dramatist seems to be doing his utmost to glorify the great national hero of Agincourt, inserting paeans of praise through the mouth of an all too idealistic, or flattering, Chorus, but he regularly undercuts those paeans from act to act by unmasking the Machiavellian character of the king and his doubtful right not only to invade France but even to rule over England. So now with *Henry VIII*, unlike any of the other plays attributed to Shakespeare in the First Folio, we are presented with a series of impressive pageants amid which the least impressive character is that of the king himself—as of a human figure without a face, which is by no means what one has come to expect of Shakespeare!

One of the first to draw attention to this discrepancy in *Henry VIII* was the great Dr. Johnson, with his famous comment that "the genius of Shakespeare comes in and goes out with Catherine [*sic*]". It was only later in the mid-nineteenth century that the proposal was made, by James Spedding and others, to divide the play between Shakespeare himself and a collaborator, who was identified as the young and promising dramatist for the King's Men, John Fletcher. With him Shakespeare seems to have collaborated not only in *Henry VIII* but also in *Two Noble Kinsmen* and (the missing) *Cardenio*, which were both attributed from the beginning to Shakespeare and Fletcher together. Characteristic of the known plays of Fletcher is precisely that emphasis on spectacle and pageant, with an addiction to feminine endings, which one notices in *Henry VIII* more than in any other of Shakespeare's plays. In particular, those scenes towards the end of the play, in Acts IV and V, featuring Archbishop Cranmer and his glowing prophecy of the future reign of the newborn Princess Elizabeth, indebted as they are to John Foxe's *Book of Martyrs* (1563)—to which Shakespeare was otherwise never indebted—are generally seen to proceed from the pen of the younger dramatist.

In contrast to the seemingly blissful ending, with all happiness promised to the uxorious king, his beautiful young wife, and his baby princess—a happiness that is undermined by the historical events which occurred in the immediate future—the play begins with a Prologue, and its ominous warning, "I come no more to make you laugh. Things now, / That bear a weighty and a serious brow, / Sad, high, and working, full of state and woe, / Such noble scenes as make the eye to flow, / We now present." Such words produce in the minds of the audience an expectation that the play to follow is to be a tragedy on "the great matter" of King Henry VIII's divorce from Queen Katharine, whereas the eventual coronation of the new Queen Anne Boleyn and the solemn christening of the baby Princess Elizabeth by Archbishop Cranmer stand in contradiction to what we have been led to expect—as if another, inferior dramatist, who is hardly interested in what has gone before, has taken over.

Then in the course of the play there follow a succession of what in mediaeval terms would be called "the falls of princes". First comes the sad downfall of the great Duke of Buckingham, convicted on the bare word of a servant, though his real fault consists in his greatness—and his better claim to the English throne than the king himself. Then there is Queen Katharine herself, whose only fault is not to have pleased the king better by providing him with a male heir. And then there is the great Cardinal Wolsey, who has been somehow responsible for the two preceding downfalls and who is now at fault—ironically like the queen—for not having pleased the king better by securing the desired divorce from Rome on Henry's behalf. In each of these downfalls it is the king himself who appears as chiefly responsible, while in each of them it also appears that the victim is relatively innocent. Yet out of them all the king strangely emerges not as villain but as victor, rewarded with the enchanting wife of his dreams and a baby princess concerning whom great things are prophesied—though he still lacks the male heir he has expected from his former wife, and for which lack he has divorced her.

Also strangely enough, in contrast to what was even in Shakespeare's time generally known about the reign of Henry VIII, there is no mention made of the tragic end of Anne Boleyn—when she was accused of adultery and executed for treason in the very year, 1536, when her former rival Katharine of Aragon died under mysterious circumstances (it was rumoured, of poisoning at the hands of Anne) in her retirement at Kimbolton. Nor is any mention made of the religious changes undertaken by Henry VIII, beginning with his assumption of the claim to be supreme head of the Church of England, and going on to the dissolution of all the monasteries and shrines in his kingdom—all of them dating within the time of the play. Such silence is surely more eloquent than words!

As for Katharine, her characterization, like that of Henry himself, is to be found not so much in this play as in the preceding *Winter's Tale.* In this respect we may note a strange, ironical contrast between the boastful claim in the subtitle of *Henry VIII, All is True,* which for a drama is somewhat self-contradictory, and the humble, self-deprecating title of *The Winter's Tale,* whose happy outcome is commented upon by Paulina as something that, "Were it but told you, should be hooted at / Like an old tale" (v.3). So when we turn from Henry to Leontes, and from Katharine to Hermione, we find them both strangely coming to life, as in that "miracle" of resurrection which Paulina produces out of the seeming statue of Hermione at the end of the play. In *Henry VIII* the frenzy of Leontes is not depicted, as Henry can find nothing in the nature of adultery of which to accuse Katharine, only he has doubts concerning the validity of their marriage—or rather the original papal dispensation. On the other hand, there is a noticeable continuity between the characterization of Hermione and that of Katharine when it comes to their respective trials, at which they both defend themselves with dignity, as daughters of great kings, before they go on to appeal to the religious authority, whether of the god Apollo at Delphos or of the Pope at Rome.

Even so, in the distribution of scenes made by Spedding and other scholars between Shakespeare and Fletcher, not all those featuring Katharine are ascribed to Shakespeare, but Fletcher is assigned not a few of them, including the affecting final scene. Even here, however, to Shakespeare evidently belong the unusually detailed stage directions concerning

Katharine's vision of "personages, clad in white robes, wearing on their heads garlands of bays", who also present her with a garland. They are not angels, as is often assumed, but martyrs, as described in the Apocalypse (Rev 12:10), implying that Katharine is shortly to be received into their number. On the other hand, her rival Anne Boleyn, who has displaced her as Henry's second queen, is by no means so favourably presented. Rather, she is sharply criticized in conversations with a mysterious Old Lady as dishonest, with more than a spice of hypocrisy and a "soft cheveril conscience"—that is, a pliant, easily stretched conscience—and ambitious, with an eye on the crown, for all her oaths that "I would not be a queen / For all the world" (ii.3). Moreover, while Katharine's end is ideally depicted, even if at Fletcher's hands, Anne's—despite the common knowledge of the fate that befell her in the very year of Katharine's death—is covered up in silence. Even without the now well established hypothesis of collaboration, one's appreciation of the play as a whole—as of *Henry V*—is undermined by the ironical contrast between what we are shown in the play, for all its boast that "all is true", and what we know from the historical records. But with the hypothesis we come to realize that the irony is mainly on Shakespeare's side, leaving the younger Fletcher in blissful ignorance of the truth.

Then there is a final irony concerning the play on the occasion of its first performance on the feast of SS. Peter and Paul, June 29, 1613, when a spark from the firing of a cannon ignited the straw on the roof of the Globe Theatre and burnt the whole house down. Was it an accident, or a deliberate case of arson? There were different theories even at the time. Anyhow, it is what the dramatist himself seems to have prophesied in Prospero's famous speech at the end of his last complete play, *The Tempest,* concerning "The cloud-capp'd towers, the gorgeous palaces, / The solemn temples, the great Globe itself", all of which "shall dissolve, / And, like this insubstantial pageant" (of *Henry VIII*) "faded, / Leave not a rack behind" (iv.1). And so, we may add, Shakespeare brought his dramatic career to a dramatic and fiery end.

chapter 8

The Last Heroine

Miranda in *The Tempest*

LIKE THE EARLY comedies of *Love's Labour's Lost* and *A Midsummer Night's Dream*, Shakespeare's final tragi-comedy of *The Tempest* seems to have been mostly of his own devising. Only for the initial tempest and the prevailing inspiration of the play he evidently owed much to contemporary accounts of the shipwreck of *The Sea-Venture* on the coast of the Bermudas, one of nine ships sailing from England in 1609 for the relief of the colony of Virginia. The locality of the shipwreck is even mentioned in the text of the play, in Ariel's reference to "the still-vex'd Bermoothes" (i.2). But to conclude from this brief mention and the circumstances surrounding the composition of the play that this is Shakespeare's first drama on the New World in America, or that it is a satire on European colonization, is going too far in the postmodernist tendency to read the present into the past, with the doubtful benefit of "hindsight". After all, the dramatist has himself set his play in the midst of the Mediterranean on some imaginary desert island located between Tunis and Naples. That should indicate a Christian background, but owing to the restrictions imposed on him by the Act of 1606, Shakespeare's only obvious reference to religion is in his masque of pagan goddesses in Act IV for the engagement ceremony of the young couple, Prince Ferdinand and Prospero's daughter, Miranda.

Turning now to the principal characters of the play, the one who most impresses us is surely the great magician Prospero, former Duke of Milan but now banished from his duchy by his younger brother Antonio—like the exiled duke in *As You Like It*, who has also been displaced by a younger brother, Frederick. It is he who controls all the events in the play from his cell at the centre of his magic island—if with the necessary assistance of his guardian spirit, Ariel. Insofar as he has any topical reference to the dramatist's own situation in Jacobean England, he is (by common consent) Shakespeare himself. For just as he controls everything on the island with his magic wand and book of spells, so the great dramatist controls everything on the stage by means of his pen and parchment (the appropriate name of a certain pub at Stratford). And just as in the end of the play he vows, "I'll break my staff" and "I'll drown my book" (v.1), so Shakespeare may be heard through the mouth of Prospero bidding farewell to the stage in the final Epilogue.

All this, however, doesn't make Prospero the central character in his own play. He may be, in scholastic terminology, the "efficient cause", but for the "final cause" we have to turn to his daughter, Miranda, whom he assures in their opening scene together, once the artificial tempest has died down, "It has all been done for thee" (i.2). So from the outset, for all her somnolence (which may reflect that of the Jacobean audience), her father has to explain everything to her, going back to the first causes of their presence on the island. Here the emphasis of Prospero is interestingly religious, as he stresses how it was by divine providence that they arrived on this island instead of perishing in the waves, and how it was little Miranda herself, as it were his guardian angel, who kept his hopes high in face of seeming despair. And now, he adds, this same providence is sending him a ship carrying all his former enemies, if only he will make use of his magic to bring the ship to the island and his enemies to his magician's cell.

The first passenger on the ship to land on the island, however, is none of Prospero's former enemies but the son of Alonso, that King of Naples who had been confederate with Prospero's brother Antonio in the usurpation of the duchy of Milan. This is Prince Ferdinand, who now follows the strange music played by Ariel, to the tune first of "Come unto these yellow sands", then of "Full fathom five thy father lies" (i.2)—till he is brought into the presence of Miranda, while Prospero remains in the background. At once they fall in love with each other, Ferdinand seeing in her "the goddess / On whom these airs attend", and Miranda regarding him as "A thing divine, for nothing natural / I ever saw so noble." Apart from him she has known no other human being than her father and herself, since Ariel is a spirit of the air, and Caliban (Prospero's slave) is but a creature of the earth. Only Prospero, considering (with Lysander in *A Midsummer Night's Dream*) that "The course of true love never (should) run smooth" (i.2), decides to make things difficult for the young couple by treating Ferdinand as a spy. So for a time, despite all the protests of Miranda, he makes the prince his slave.

As for the other passengers, they have all come safely to the island—as Prospero has assured Miranda, in Pauline terms, "There is no soul, / No, not so much perdition as an hair, / Betid to any creature in the vessel" (i.2, cf. Acts 27:34)—but some of them have different ways of seeing things from others. There are the idealists, like the old counsellor Gonzalo, who see nothing but enchantment in the island, and there are the realists, like Prospero's brother Antonio and Alonso's brother Sebastian (a pair of names oddly coming together out of another shipwreck in the earlier *Twelfth Night*), who have nothing but complaints about their situation. As for Alonso, he tends to agree with the realists, only he is too preoccupied with the loss of his son Ferdinand to join in their complaints. Gonzalo, however, strives to keep their spirits up by entertaining them with his "merry fooling", in the form of speculations on an ideal commonwealth which he would like to establish on the island. In his detailed description scholars have found interesting parallels with the essays of Montaigne, especially that "On Cannibals" (translated into English by John Florio and published in 1603). But in its general idea and in view of the character who presents it, we may recognize the figure of that great counsellor to Henry VIII, Sir Thomas More, the witty author of that earlier commonwealth named *Utopia*—who also appears in other romances of this period, such as Belarius in *Cymbeline* and Camillo in *The Winter's Tale*. It is also noteworthy that, among all the shipwrecked passengers, he is the one who receives the warmest welcome from Prospero on their subsequent arrival in the magician's cell.

Then in Act III we are shown the maturing of the love between Ferdinand and Miranda. The very fact that, though a prince, he is made to carry logs as Prospero's slave—the kind of task otherwise entrusted to Caliban—fills the tender heart of Miranda with pity for him, and that, as Olivia tells Viola in *Twelfth Night*, is but "a degree to love" (iii.1). Naturally Miranda is already in love with him, and the sight of him suffering makes her love him all the more, while he on his side is no less ready to endure all such sufferings for the happiness of having her beside him. Then on learning her name—though in the telling of it she fears she has disobeyed her father—he exclaims, "Admir'd Miranda! / Indeed, the top of admiration, worth / What's dearest to the world!" Thus he sees in her yet another of Shakespeare's ideal heroines described in traditional terms of devotion to the Virgin Mary. He conceives her not only as "full of grace", in contrast to the courtly women he has known back in Naples, but also in connection with two titles from the traditional "Litany of Loreto", in which Mary is addressed both as *"Mater admirabilis"* and as *"Virgo veneranda."* Also, by virtue of her name Miranda is paired with that earlier romantic heroine Marina, "born at sea" (with an echo of the other title, *Stella Maris*).

Meanwhile, the purpose of Prospero in keeping the other passengers together, apart from Ferdinand, is realized when Ariel leads them to a certain place on the island and addresses them in solemn tones as "three men of sin", namely, Alonso, Sebastian, and Antonio. This purpose is not so much one of revenge as rather to bring them to repentance for the wrong they have committed against Prospero—such repentance as we see more impressively in the case of Leontes in *The Winter's Tale*. For without repentance (as Claudius recognizes in his soliloquy in *Hamlet* iii.3) there can be no true forgiveness. In solemn tones, therefore, Ariel warns them, echoing the words of St. Ignatius in the exercise on sin in *The Spiritual Exercises*, "The powers, delaying, not forgetting, have / Incens'd the seas and shores, yea, all the creatures, / Against your peace" (iii.3). So now, he adds, for them to avoid such perdition there remains "nothing but heart-sorrow / And a clear life ensuing"—which is like Hamlet's warning to his mother, "Confess yourself to heaven, / Repent what's past, avoid what is to come" (iii.4). For all their solemnity, however, the words of Ariel are strangely ineffective. All they do is to induce in Alonso a deep sleep, of which the other two men of sin are about to take immediate advantage by killing him—but they are anticipated by Ariel, who wakes up the other sleeping passengers.

All this time the dramatist has been developing a subplot centred on Prospero's other servant, the earthy islander Caliban (whose name is a metathesis for the tribes of cannibals in the West Indies called Caribs), with two drunken sailors from the shipwreck, Trinculo and Stephano. It is his plan to avail himself of their assistance to take his revenge on his hated master by killing him and thus gaining his freedom—though his contradictory idea of freedom goes with a willing slavery to Stephano as the god who keeps him supplied with liquor (from the ship). Now, while promising to reward the two sailors with all the natural assets of the island known to him, he first leads them to Prospero's cell for the essential goal of murder—from which they are continually being distracted by one thing and another. But with such comic characters lined up against Prospero, we have no fear for the magician's safety, so long as everything on the island is under the supervision of Ariel.

Then in Act IV we have the provisional climax to the love story between Ferdinand and Miranda in the engagement ceremony arranged for them by Prospero—in anticipation of their formal (presumably Christian) wedding back in Naples. First he insists (as it were echoing the previous vows between Florizel and Perdita in *The Winter's Tale*) on the importance of Ferdinand's respecting the virginity of Miranda till the night of their wedding in Naples. Then, on Ferdinand's solemn assurance to this effect, as central to the engagement, he proceeds to show them "Some vanity of mine art" in the form of a masque of spirits under the direction of Ariel (iv.1). Unlike the preceding romances, however, here is no pagan theophany (if with Christian correspondences), whether of the goddess Diana in *Pericles*, or the god Jupiter in *Cymbeline*, or Apollo's oracle in *The Winter's Tale*, but only of spirits acting the parts of the goddesses Iris, Ceres, and Juno, and at the end of the masque they all vanish "to a strange, hollow, and confused noise". The language of the masque, too, for all its artificial elaboration, is (as Prospero has admitted) merely "vanity"—such as Shakespeare might have delegated to the inferior genius of Ben Jonson, the expert in courtly masques.

Once the masque is over, however, and the spirits disappear, on Prospero's sudden realization that Caliban and his drunken allies are approaching his cell, Shakespeare again takes over with his dramatic genius. Not that Prospero has had any need to worry, as all has been left in the capable hands of Ariel. But now, as he perceives the anxiety on the faces of the couple before him, he provides them no longer with a "vanity of mine art" but with his (and Shakespeare's) humanist philosophy. "Our revels now are ended", he assures them. "These our actors, / As I foretold you, were all spirits and / Are melted into air, into thin air." In the same way, he continues, everything around them—not so much the sights on the island as what one might see from a barge on the river Thames, all the impressive buildings of London, including "the great Globe itself"—will dissolve and "Leave not a rack behind". And so, he concludes, in words that are inscribed on the scroll held in the hands of the sculpted Shakespeare in the Poets' Corner of Westminster Abbey, "We are such stuff / As dreams are made on, and our little life / Is rounded with a sleep."

Here is, one may feel, the great poet-dramatist-philosopher's mature comment on human life in what he intends to be his final play before retiring from the stage and returning home to Stratford. But, we may well wonder, does he really mean to say that human life is nothing but a dream, or that it is "rounded with a sleep", and that there is nothing more substantial to it than that? In this speech, we may note, he is speaking of material things, which we see with our eyes, whether on a lonely island or in the crowded city of London. Then it is insofar as men remain on that level of merely outward appearances, that they are "such stuff as dreams are made on", and such a life is indeed "rounded with a sleep", considering that dreams occur to the mind or imagination of man only while he is asleep. But is that all? Prospero himself doesn't seem to advert to the question. Only, he is speaking to the young lovers after an engagement ceremony in which he has earnestly insisted on Ferdinand's respect for the virginity of Miranda up till the time of their wedding in Naples. Then he himself can return to Milan, where "Every third thought shall be my grave" (v.1). Does he really mean, we may ask, that all these things, love, marriage, and death, are just as transitory as the material buildings to be seen on the banks of the river Thames? Surely not! Rather, as the poet says in his sonnets on love, "So long as men can breathe, or eyes can see, / So long lives this, and this gives life to thee" (xviii), and "Let me not to the marriage of true minds / Admit impediment" (cxvi), and "Poor soul, the centre of my sinful earth. . . . And Death once dead, there's no more dying then" (cxlvi).

Anyhow, this isn't yet the end of the play. The noble passengers have yet to be escorted by Ariel to Prospero's cell, where they are left in an immobile, unconscious condition. Prospero readily resolves, if at the urging of Ariel, to pardon his enemies, considering that "the rarer action is / In virtue than in vengeance" (v.1)—in this following the example of Cymbeline, who also says at the end of his play, "Pardon's the word to all" (v.5). Yet of his three old enemies only one has been brought to repentance, as much for the imagined loss of his son as out of sorrow for his sin against Prospero. Now, as his prisoners gradually come to their senses, Prospero greets the holy old man Gonzalo, who helped to preserve him at the time of his banishment from Milan. Then the others, on coming to their senses, are amazed at what they see, especially as Prospero now sees fit to wear his former ducal robes. Alonso, however, is still grieving over the loss of his dear son, lamenting, "Irreparable is the loss, and Patience / Says it is past her cure", to which Prospero somewhat enigmatically responds, "I rather think / You have not sought her help, of whose soft grace / For the like loss I have her sovereign aid, / And rest myself content." Of which lady is he here speaking? The goddess Patience (as in *Twelfth Night* ii.4, or in *Pericles* v.1), or perhaps the Virgin Mary, or both? Then a curtain is drawn, to reveal Ferdinand and Miranda playing each other at a game of chess, which causes yet more wonder among the visitors. "A most high miracle!" exclaims Sebastian, in an unexpected change of mood. But it is Miranda who feels most wonder at the sight of so many noble visitors, and this prompts her to exclaim, in words that are often taken as the keynote to the whole play, "O wonder! / How many goodly creatures are there here! / How beauteous mankind is! O brave new world, / That has such people in't!"

Thus does Shakespeare bring his last play to an end—as he does the other tragi-comic romances of his final period—on a note of "miracle", "wonder", "the supernatural", "providence"—though it is rather in his subjective mind (as in the mind of Miranda) than in the objective reality of Jacobean England. As for his own personal affairs, now is the time for him to retire from the stage and return home to his family in Stratford where, like Prospero in Milan, "Every third thought shall be my grave". And so, when Prospero comes forward to pronounce the Epilogue, we may be sure it is the dramatist speaking through the mouth of the magician—as he may well have in fact been playing the part of Prospero. Now, he says, without his dramatic art (or magic craft) to support him any longer, "My ending is despair, / Unless I be reliev'd by prayer, / Which pierces so that it assaults / Mercy itself and frees all faults." His is, in other words, the prayer of the humble man which, as he has read in Ecclesiasticus, "goeth through the clouds, and ceaseth not till it come near, and will not depart till the most High have respect thereunto" (35:17). There before the mercy throne of God, as he has (in the person of Prospero) forgiven his enemies, even without waiting for their repentance, so he hopes to be forgiven his sins. And so he humbly asks pardon from his audience, as he also hopes for pardon from God. It is a religious ending (comparable to that of Chaucer at the end of his *Canterbury Tales*) to a deeply religious, if seemingly secular, dramatic career.

There only remains a further question. Why at such an early age, a mere forty-six years, should the dramatist have decided to quit the stage and return home? Has he by now lost all interest in his dramatic work? Or does he murmur to himself, in the words of his dirge for Imogen in *Cymbeline*, "Thou thy worldly task hast done" (iv.2). Or is he now longing to devote his remaining years to his wife, Anne Hathaway, and his Papist daughter, Susanna—though perhaps less to his wayward younger daughter, Judith? Certainly, the prevalence of ideal heroines in his final romances, as well of good doctors (perhaps modelled on Susanna's husband, Dr. John Hall), may well point to this last-mentioned possibility.

Still, we know of two events that occurred shortly before the first performance of *The Tempest* that may have influenced Shakespeare's decision to retire. First, there is evidence of two recent plays of his, *King Lear* and *Pericles*, being performed on the basis of their quarto editions of 1608 and 1609 (respectively) by a group of recusant players under the patronage of Sir Richard Cholmeley before audiences at recusant houses in the West Riding of Yorkshire during the winter season of 1609–10. These performances became a subject of scandal, owing to an interlude ridiculing Protestant ministers, and it was soon brought to the attention of the Court of Star Chamber at Westminster. Secondly, in 1611 the Protestant historian John Speed published his *History of Great Britain*, in which, while defending the injured reputation of the Lollard martyr Sir John Oldcastle, he associated the Jesuit Robert Persons with the dramatist William Shakespeare, as "the papist and his poet", for the way they had both ridiculed Oldcastle under the name of Sir John Falstaff. Maybe it was in the face of such unfavourable publicity, with which the crypto-Catholic dramatist saw his "cover" being blown, that he felt it would be dangerous for him to stay longer in London, and advisable for him to return to more sympathetic surroundings in his native Stratford and the nearby Forest of Arden.

Finally, apart from occasional collaboration with the young dramatist of his former company, the King's Men, Shakespeare bows out of "this great stage of fools" (*King Lear* iv.6) except for two significant matters which may serve to justify much of what has been said in the foregoing pages, first the fact of his purchase of the Blackfriars Gatehouse, a notorious hiding-place for Catholic recusants, in 1613, and secondly the tradition, recorded by an Anglican clergyman, Richard Davies, in the late seventeenth century, that "he died a papist", that is to say, in 1616.

chapter 9
The Greatness of Shakespeare in the Jacobean Plays

Now that we have dwelt on each of the plays composed by Shakespeare for the King's Men during the new reign of James I, it is time for us to stand back and view them as a whole. Then perhaps we may catch some glimpse of what T. S. Eliot calls "the pattern in Shakespeare's carpet". The question we have now to put before ourselves is that of greatness, or genius. In what does the dramatic genius of Shakespeare consist in all these plays taken together? How does he achieve greatness in them, almost (one may think) in spite of himself? What is the source (one may even say, the supernatural source) of his ever-flowing inspiration, in which it seems there is no authorial complaint of "writer's block"? It is indeed a mystery, all but overwhelming when we look back over these plays in their unending variety, combined with their immeasurable profundity. It is a mystery which obliges us to return to them once more, this time not so much in generalities, which fail to do justice to the dramatist's unique originality, as in a recapitulation of the main points of each play till we see them converging upon one point at the heart of Shakespeare's genius.

First, there is the dramatist's inimitable faculty of reading the source story or play, such as Cinthio's tale of the Moor and the Ensign, which is the starting point of *Othello*. The story itself is impressive enough, and as such it no doubt appealed to the mind of the dramatist. But then, as he put his heart into what he read, he succeeded in breathing life into its characters one by one. First, there is the Moor, as an unusual type (to an Englishman of that age) of Everyman. Yet the more unusual the characterization of the type, the more impressive he becomes as a human being. He may be a "blackamoor", but he is of "royal siege", a trusted general in the service of Venice, a man of mature integrity who can almost say, with Jesus to his adversaries, "Which of you shall convict me of sin?" (Jn 8:46). At the same time, deep down in our hearts we may recognize something like him, or something dangerously close to him. For as he is Everyman, he is each one of us, and so of him we may say, "There but for the grace of God go I!" Such is Shakespeare's skill in characterizing Othello as to bring him close to us, and ourselves correspondingly close to him. Even while we watch the play enacted on the stage, or read the text of the play in our study, we are unconsciously fulfilling the axiom of Aristotle, *"Omnis cognoscens cognoscendo fit quodammodo cognitum"*—Every knower in the act of knowing somehow becomes the object known. That is, we become one with Othello, particularly in his moments of dramatic intensity.

Then, what about the Ensign, who under Shakespeare's hands becomes the villain Iago, and whose character has been drawn no less impressively than that of Othello? He may, as he suggests more than once in the course of the play, be presented as "the worser spirit", or tempting devil, such as we find endlessly multiplied in the fantastic statuary of mediaeval churches, whose sculptors seem to have found more inspiration in the carving of devils than of saints or angels. Yet Shakespeare's Iago is no grotesque caricature, like the gargoyles on Notre Dame in Paris. He is too alarmingly real, even a typical English gentleman, with two sides to his character—one the scheming side, which he reveals in his soliloquies and occasionally in conversation with his pal Roderigo, and the other the honest, prudently advising side, which he reveals to Cassio and Othello. He thus uncomfortably reminds us of the old English saying that "the devil is a gentleman". Nowhere do these two sides of his come together so impressively as in the great scene of temptation, on which Milton may well have drawn for his representation of Satan's temptation of Eve in Book VIII of *Paradise Lost*.

In this play, in the order of their appearances as presented by the dramatist, first comes the villain, who manifests his prosaic villainy in his self-revealing, yet all-concealing conversation with Roderigo—as the standard of Satan is revealed and concealed, according to St. Ignatius's meditation on the Two Standards, under a screen of smoke (or today, one might add, a smog-filled city). He in turn leads us into the presence of Othello, thus sharing the honour of betrayer with his henchman Roderigo, after they have together betrayed the fact of Othello's clandestine marriage with Desdemona to her father Brabantio. Then at last we are introduced, in the order of a mediaeval procession, to the sacred presence of Desdemona, with Othello's solemn account of how he wooed and won her, as Everyman making her his "better angel".

In this processional order we see the dramatist pointing, ever so subtly, to the secret of his inspiration as well in this as in his subsequent Jacobean plays. There is nothing like it in all his previous Elizabethan plays, certainly not in Hamlet's Ophelia, nor even in the lady Portia—though of all the Elizabethan plays it may be said that *The Merchant of Venice* comes closest in plot and character as well as theme to *Othello*. More than any other heroine, whether in the previous Elizabethan age or the present Jacobean age, it is surely Desdemona who most approximates to the mediaeval ideal of the Blessed Virgin Mary, both for her fullness of grace (as hailed in Cassio's words) and for her readiness as "advocate" to intercede for poor sinners (like Cassio). Nor is it enough for her to be compared to the Virgin Mary, even by such characters as Roderigo (who cannot but recognize this truth in her) and Iago (who merely uses it as a means of tempting Cassio to the destruction of both him and Othello). But in the final scene of murder, when Othello has unconsciously taken over the configuration of Judas from Iago, Desdemona appears as a figure not only of the Virgin Mary, but also of the innocent Christ on the cross. There within Shakespeare's dramatization of Cinthio's tale we find a further confluence of two dramatic traditions from the Middle Ages, those of the morality play of *Everyman* and the mystery plays of the Passion.

In this way the spectator of the play on stage, or the reader of the text in his study, may well—insofar as he really enters into the action of the play—say to himself not just "I am Othello!" (inasmuch as Othello is recognized as Everyman), but even "I am Christ!" (whom Othello also conceives himself to be from the first scene in which he appears), and then, more fearfully in the further progression of the play, "I am Judas!" This may even lead up to the eternal question, which few academic critics are prepared to face, "How can I hope for salvation?" or "Does nothing await me after death but eternal damnation in the depth of hell?" To this question the temptation of Iago has led us, all unsuspectingly, and we are caught in the devil's trap. So we are left by Iago with the sneering words, "From this time forth I never will speak word." But neither for Othello nor for us is that the last word, since there remains the dead form of Desdemona, offered in sacrifice for her husband and for us. Then Othello catches her up and kisses her, and in that embrace he is symbolically restored to life, before he dies.

Also when we turn to *King Lear* we come upon the same basic pattern, with a difference of detail. Needless to say, there is no temptation of Lear from without. All is from within, from his own rash, impulsive nature—as with his near namesake in *The Winter's Tale*, Leontes. Immediately he is disappointed at the unflattering, honest response of his true daughter, Cordelia, and her "Nothing" elicits from him only the cruelly punishing pun of Aristotle's axiom, "Nothing will come of nothing." So, already like Christ, she is forsaken by her own father and despised among men, in words (uttered by France) that explicitly relate her to the Man of Sorrows. All the same, she is from the outset the "better angel" to this other Everyman, her father, of whom his daughter Regan cruelly if truly remarks, "He hath ever but slenderly known himself." Cordelia is his grace, his wisdom, and in her banishment all he has in return is *perdita gratia* (a loss of grace like that indicated in the name of the similarly banished daughter of Leontes, Perdita), as well as his folly in the personified form of the Fool. Then what with the folly of the Fool and the madness of the mock beggar Edgar, Lear not only is driven to madness himself amid the misery of the storm, but also returns to himself with the symbolic return of Cordelia—who here represents the welcoming father of Christ's parable in relation to her father as prodigal son.

In the foregoing remarks I haven't said so much about the villains in the play, or about the double plot, which is an addition and complication in *King Lear* to the comparatively simple plot of *Othello*. In the primary plot of Lear and Cordelia we have not one but two villains, his daughters and her sisters, Goneril and Regan, who conspire to drive their father out into the pitiless storm, as it were a reflection in the world of Nature of their own pitiless hearts. They even conspire to kill him—though in the outcome they kill only themselves. Unlike Iago, however, they aren't temptresses. They merely take advantage of the convenient opportunity which their fond foolish father puts into their hands to get rid of him as occasion offers. In the secondary plot, however, between the old Earl of Gloucester and his sons, Edgar and Edmund, it is the bastard Edmund who is, like Iago, the contriver of villainy against both his father and his brother. His temptation works all too easily on his gullible father, and he is instrumental not only in the banishment of his good brother but also in the terrible blinding of his father by Regan's ruthless husband, Cornwall, and eventually in the cruel hanging of Cordelia in prison.

Such an outcome is no less cruel than anything perpetrated by Iago on Othello and Desdemona, and it is cruelly depicted in the culminating moment of the final scene, when the old Lear comes tottering on stage bearing the dead body of Cordelia and crying, "How, howl, howl, howl!" (v.3). It is so pitiful, and our hearts bleed rather for the poor old man in his grief than for the dead daughter, who is now beyond grief. Yet in the eyes of a Christian audience, for whom we may suppose the play was originally composed by the Christian playwright, the excited words of Albany, "O, see, see!" point not only to this tableau of the sorrowing father with the dead body of his innocent daughter, but also to the *Pieta*, that monument (whether in sculpture or in painting) of the sorrowing mother with the dead body of her innocent Son, which was familiar to all worshippers in churches of pre-Reformation England. Here, more than ever before in the play, more than anything even in *Othello*, coming on top of a series of side-piercing sights evoked by the episode when the side of Christ is pierced by the soldier's spear, the ideal heroine is presented as a figure of Christ the redeemer—in dramatic fulfilment of the prophecy of Zechariah, "They shall look upon him whom they have pierced." (Zech 12:10, Jn 19:37).

Then, if Lear is indeed Everyman, we may well reflect on him, as on Othello, "I am Lear." Only, there is no such problem about the damnation of Lear as there seems to be about Othello. After all, Othello had up to his dying moment condemned himself to the lowest depth of hell, with Judas. It was, however, at that moment, in his dying kiss of Desdemona, that we obtain a glimpse of his salvation, saved by the intercession of her whose advocacy continues beyond the grave. As for Lear, though in his mad grief he killed the slave that was hanging Cordelia, he comes in the end to see the breath of life stirring on her lips. So when he dies embracing her, he is all unconsciously a reflection of the Blessed Mother in her heartbroken sorrow. Here surely is the message Shakespeare wishes to convey, if unconsciously, to his unsuspecting audience—a message not of black despair, which is all the agnostic critic can see, but of hope against hope, as of a gleam of sunlight appearing through the darkest storm-clouds.

This may seem to represent the utmost of what Shakespeare's dramatic art can be expected to achieve, built as it is not just on the shifting sand of stories borrowed from Renaissance *novelle* or mediaeval chronicles, but on the rock foundation of the simpler morality and mystery plays, looking at once to men of all ages and nations and to Christ himself with his mother Mary as new Man and new Woman in the new Christian era. At the same time, throughout his dramatic career Shakespeare alternates between the opposites of tragedy (or tragic history) and comedy, as it were requiring relief from the stern seriousness of the one in the merry laughter of the other. In this respect he is like the weather in England, as described by the Gentleman who says of Cordelia on her return to rescue her poor father, "You have seen / Sunshine and rain at once. Her smiles and tears / Were like, a better way." So here, in the first two years of the new Jacobean reign, by the side of *Othello* we have *Measure for Measure*, as the two plays for 1604, and by the side of *King Lear* we have *All's Well That Ends Well*, as the two plays for 1605. Then, if with Othello as a black, mature Everyman we have Desdemona as his "better angel", and if with Lear as a white, wizened Everyman we have the other "better angel" in Cordelia, so in their contemporary comedies we have as angelic heroines the pure novice Isabella, whom Lucio holds "as a thing ensky'd and sainted", and the pilgrim worker of miracles Helena.

Only, unlike the two tragedies, it is difficult for us to identify a suitable hero in the two comedies. In the earlier play the duke-friar, Vincentio-Lodowick, might seem to qualify (like Prospero in *The Tempest*), but friars aren't supposed to be heroes—though as duke, Vincentio does propose to Isabella at the end of the play, without obtaining any response from her. There is something even overwhelming about Vincentio, who seems to fulfil the conditions not so much for Everyman as for divine providence. So it is the role of the would-be villain, Lord Angelo, to bring out the better part of Isabella as Angel of Mercy—though her identification, whether as Mary or as Christ, is uncertain. Bertram, however, as prodigal husband, is too weakly drawn, with the insipid Parolles—all too easily forgotten—as Vice of Prodigality at his side, making such an odd contrast with that other figure of Prodigality, Sir John Falstaff. Helena, however, stands out all the more vividly in her configuration with the Virgin Mary, both in her miraculous cure of the French king (recalling the contemporary miracles of the Virgin in the Low Countries) and in her supposed pilgrimage to the shrine of St. James (the holy Iago) at Compostela in Spain. As for a parallelism with *King Lear*, it appears most in their common dramatization of the parable of the prodigal son, where in the tragedy it is a prodigal father, and in the comedy a prodigal husband, with the place of the father taken in the one case by the daughter and in the other by the wife.

Anyhow, putting ourselves as it were in Shakespeare's shoes, after his completion of these four plays of 1604 and 1605, we may ask, echoing Cordelia, "Now what is poor Shakespeare to do?" What more can he produce for English audiences out of his tragic or comic genius? That is a question to which he gives a preliminary, if unsatisfactory, answer in his next tragedy, *Macbeth*. Such a famous, such a great tragedy indeed, and yet so singularly dissatisfying! It seems to have been put together so hastily, out of bits and pieces left over from previous attempts. First, there is the possible visit of the dramatist to Edinburgh in the aftermath of the Essex rebellion of 1601 and his composition of *Hamlet*, considering how much closer *Macbeth* is to that play than either *Othello* or *King Lear*. Then, there is the further possibility of his having refurbished it as an appropriate play for the King's Men to celebrate the arrival of the new King James I in his capital of London, only to have to put it on hold by an outbreak of the plague. Thirdly, in the aftermath of the Gunpowder Plot and the trials of the plotters, there is the sudden need of a play for the entertainment of King Christian IV of Denmark in August 1606. One may, therefore, suppose that this was what the dramatist put together at the last moment, hoping the kings would at least be satisfied by the brevity of the performance.

Anyhow, the important thing to bear in mind about *Macbeth* and its difference from the preceding Jacobean tragedies is that between it and them fell the dark shadow of the Gunpowder Plot. Not that Shakespeare (as is too often given out by scholars) felt the same horror at the actions of the plotters as that felt by Macduff on discovering the dead body of Duncan. After all, what had the plotters done? Nothing— apart from playing into the hands of the government to whom they were but as puppets. Long before the so-called discovery of the plot on November 5, Shakespeare would have been aware of what was going on, as most of the plotters were neighbours and relatives of his from the region of the Forest of Arden, and many of them, including his cousin Robert Catesby, were frequenters of the Mermaid Tavern in London, which was also frequented by Shakespeare himself and Ben Jonson (who was even implicated in the plot).

As for the play itself, which took its ill-omened rise out of such circumstances, it may bear a superficial resemblance to *Othello*, in that it also has a single tragic plot which bears the hero-villain onwards from the triple prophecy of the witches in the beginning till he encounters his doom at the end. But the deeper difference lies in this very designation of Macbeth as at once both hero and villain—like Richard III. What is more, the one lady in the play who might seem to have been cast as heroine, by his side as hero, is no less smeared in blood-guilt and no less in league with the "murdering ministers" of the air than the witches. It may be conventional to call them hero and heroine, but they are rather a pair of villains. Then because Macbeth, unlike Othello, has no "better angel" to intercede for him in the tragic outcome, the play, which is still as much of a morality play as the other, has to be termed "a morality play of damnation"—in which Lady Macbeth goes her way "by self and violent hands" while Macbeth insists on shedding the blood of others up till the end. In this end, however, we have to recognize that what is tragic for Macbeth and his lady turns out to be tragi-comic, as a happy ending for Scotland. Then the abounding of sin under the bloody tyrant brings an abounding of grace, thanks to the combined efforts of two gracious kings, Malcolm and Edward, in avenging the murder of a third gracious king, Malcolm's father, Duncan.

It is no doubt the grace of these three kings, as it were in place of an ideal heroine for the personification of grace, that eventually triumphs over the evil of Macbeth and his lady, and even saves the play itself as a work of dramatic art. There is, however, no such grace to be found in the subsequent "Greek" play of *Timon of Athens*. Here it is as if the dramatist has returned to the vomit spewed forth by the indignant Lear against the ingratitude of his daughters, ignoring the unpleasant truth that he has himself been the cause of it all by his foolish preference of their flattery over Cordelia's plain truth. Still, Lear at least comes through the school of adversity to repent of his folly, with such schoolmasters as his Fool and the mad beggar. But Timon, in withdrawing from the ungrateful city to the lonely seashore, has no such schoolmaster, except that "nothing" which he finally comes to realize "brings me all things". So he dies, with no friends to mourn over him, apart from the ineffectual Alcibiades, and with no heroine to intercede for him, apart from Alcibiades' two mistresses, who are interested only in his gold. Still, there is just a suggestion that, like Jesus, he has been betrayed by his Judas-like friends who share his last supper. And that is all. It is a strange play—but not so strangely left unfinished.

Then come the two "Roman" plays, *Antony and Cleopatra* and *Coriolanus*, which are so highly praised by T. S. Eliot as works of dramatic art, but which fall short of Shake-speare's art as measured by his other Jacobean plays. In the first place, what, it may be asked, is *Antony and Cleopatra* but a dramatization of the amour between "the ne'er lust-wearied Antony", who is ready to spend the whole world upon his selfish lust, and her whom he himself terms "the triple turn'd whore", Cleopatra? From this point of view, which is objectively presented in the play, the love between the hero and the heroine—in contrast not only to the love of the preceding pairs Romeo and Juliet, Claudio and Hero, Claudio and Juliet, but also to that of Othello and Desde-mona—is nothing but a glorification of adultery and sui-cide. All in this play is on the surface. It has no depth like *King Lear*. There is nothing of Everyman in Antony, nor can Cleopatra be called his "better angel", but she is rather his "worser spirit", whose leading he follows (as in the inglori-ous outcome of Actium) to his own and her destruction. Still less is there anything in them of the new Man or the new Woman, though Antony fondly imagines their love as envisaging "new heaven, new earth", or an Elysium "where souls do couch on flowers". Yet on such love as theirs the dramatist has, it seems, poured forth, or one might say pros-tituted, his genius.

It may, therefore, have been in revulsion to it all that Shakespeare went on to limit his dramatic scope to the sim-pler, if fiercer, tragedy of *Coriolanus* in the setting of ancient Roman history. Here again, as in *Timon of Athens*, he vents his feelings of indignation at the ingratitude of the people, while withdrawing as well from those people as from the three women, his mother, his wife, and her friend, with whom—unlike Timon—he retains some connection. So the most meaningful words in this play of strident abuse are those in which he breaks off his connection with his mother, in the very act of granting her appeal for Rome, "O, mother, mother! / What have you done?"

But then, out of this strange period in which Shakespeare brings out a series of plays without a suitable heroine, he produces his final "romances" as with the wave of a magic wand—even out of the "mouldy tale" of *Pericles*. The dramatist even goes out of his way to make it more mouldy with the inclusion of ancient Gower as a kind of pop-up Chorus in between acts. He has, moreover, evidently left the awkward opening scenes of the play, taken over from George Wilkins, as he found them and developed the play in such a way as to lead up to the incredible joy of reunion for the aged hero first with his ideal daughter, Marina, then with his aged wife, Thaisa. Now at last in the person of Marina Shakespeare returns to the rich Marian associations with which he has endowed his earlier Jacobean heroines, especially Desdemona and Helena, recalling in her the Marian title "Star of the Sea" and the Marian paradox that she has now newly begotten him who formerly begot her—just as the Virgin Mary is at once daughter to the Father and mother to the Son.

Further, what Shakespeare took over in part from Wilkins for the re-enactment of the blissful reunion between Lear and Cordelia at the end of Act IV, without the supervening sorrow of Act V, he now goes on to reproduce on his own account—while incurring a further debt to his former rival and critic Robert Greene—under the mouldy title of *The Winter's Tale*. Here, too, we are introduced to an ideal heroine, Perdita, who is born to her mother in prison and straightway rejected by her father as spurious. So she is cast ashore on the lonely seacoast of Bohemia, as her father's *perdita gratia*, or lost grace—just as Cordelia was to her father Lear. Thus, unlike Pericles, it is Perdita's father,

Leontes, who is guilty both of his unjust accusation of adultery against her mother Hermione and of his subsequent rejection of Perdita. So he has to undergo a period of penance, after Hermione's trial and seeming death—a period that lasts until Perdita has grown "in grace, equal with wondering". Then on her return to her father's kingdom of Sicilia, with her lover, Prince Florizel, she brings with her both grace and wonder, in a series of reunions and reconciliations that culminate in the seeming "resurrection" of her mother—when Hermione steps down from her pedestal as a statue and resumes her human form. Such miracles in these last plays may be attributed to pagan deities, whether Apollo in this play or Diana in *Pericles*, but according to the Neo-Platonic correspondences developed by Ficino and his disciples in fifteenth-century Florence, Apollo is an alias for Christ, and Diana for the Virgin Mary.

The same motive, to reproduce the blissful scene of reunion between Lear and Cordelia, was no doubt implicit in Shakespeare's choice of yet another subject from his favourite source-book, Holinshed's *Chronicles*, in his play of *Cymbeline*, dealing with another King of Britain and his ideal daughter, Imogen. Here, too, we have the case of a heroine who has incurred the anger of her royal father, partly because (like Desdemona) she has just married the young Posthumus without her father's consent, partly because she now refuses to marry the man he has chosen for her, the unworthy son of his (unnamed) second wife. Eventually she runs away from court, though without actually being banished (like Cordelia), so as to rejoin her husband on his arrival with a Roman army in South Wales. In the end, after an immense number of amazing complications, she is reunited with him and her husband, while her stepmother has (like Lady Macbeth) committed suicide. As a whole, the play is a failure, but the dramatist evidently undertook to compose it, not just as an easy resort to Holinshed at a time when he had no other resource for dramatic composition, but rather for its promise of another happy ending under another King of Britain. To this plot he also provided a second plot on the theme of jealousy (as in *Othello*), involving Imogen's exiled husband, Posthumus, in Rome, and including the name of Iachimo as villain (as it were a little Iago). It also serves to bring out the happy ending that was denied to Othello and Desdemona by the more efficient and villainous Iago.

In these three "romances" one may well discern signs of "grouping", in terms of their happy outcome in the reunion of father and daughter, as it were in the footsteps of Lear and Cordelia. Only, in *Pericles* the original separation was not the fault of the poor father, who was but subject to an unkind Fate, whereas in the other two plays both Cymbeline and Leontes were sinfully responsible and had to repent of their sins, though Leontes shows more repentance than Cymbeline. In Shakespeare's final complete play, however, which is ironically the first of the plays presented in the First Folio of 1623, *The Tempest,* there is no such blissful reunion between father and daughter, Prospero and Miranda, for the simple reason that they have been together on their lonely island all their lives. Still, the relation between father and daughter remains important, only more importance is placed by the father himself on the other relationship between the lovers, his own daughter Miranda and the shipwrecked Prince Ferdinand, son of his former enemy, Alonso King of Naples. It is what we also find in *The Winter's Tale* between Leontes' daughter Perdita and Prince Florizel, son of his former enemy Polixenes, King of Bohemia, and in *Cymbeline* between Cymbeline's daughter Imogen and the banished Posthumus Leonatus. Moreover, in addition to the love between Ferdinand and Miranda, there is the all-important theme of repentance and forgiveness, involving Prospero in relation to his former enemies, the "three men of sin", Alonso King of Naples, his brother Sebastian, and Prospero's brother Antonio, who has usurped his place as Duke of Milan. Of them only Alonso really repents, while Sebastian's heart is moved at the "most high miracle" he sees in Prospero's cell, but Antonio remains obstinately unrepentant to the end. Yet Prospero forgives them all, just as Cymbeline in the outcome of his play declares, "Pardon's the word to all." From this viewpoint, we may well go back to *All's Well That Ends Well* as providing us with a more appropriate grouping to the last comedies, not so much as "last romances" but rather as "comedies of forgiveness". For that is the basic value of what John Vyvyan has called "the Shakespearian ethic", which is after all nothing but the Christian ethic.

Thus we are left with but one more play to complete the pattern of Shakespeare's Jacobean carpet, and that is para-doxically his incomplete part in collaboration with John Fletcher in the final history play, *Henry VIII*. This collabora-tion is, however, in no way similar to that undertaken with George Wilkins for *Pericles*. In the earlier play it seems more likely that Shakespeare simply took over from where Wilkins had left off and gave it a completion of his own devising. In the later play we have no means of saying how the two dramatists collaborated, or even how much of Fletcher's work had the approval of Shakespeare—especially considering how much in the second half of the play was dependent on a tainted source, Foxe's Protestant *Book of Martyrs*, which the older dramatist had never touched in his previous plays. His interest in the play—as Dr. Johnson per-ceptively noted—was not so much in King Henry, still less in his second queen, Anne Boleyn (who is recalled as "the wicked queen" of *Cymbeline*), as in his first wife, Katharine of Aragon. Her character, even if some of the scenes related to her have been ascribed to the pen of Fletcher, may serve as a precious clue to an inner meaning in all the previous plays of Shakespeare's Jacobean period.

First, there is the remarkably close parallel between Katharine and Hermione in *The Winter's Tale*, as also between Henry and Leontes. Then in *Cymbeline* the king is misled by his second wife, as Henry was by Anne Boleyn, both in his cruelty to Imogen, as Henry was cruel to the Princess Mary, and in his refusal to continue his payment of tribute to Rome, as Henry was prompted by his desire for a divorce to cut England off from her traditional allegiance to Rome. As for *Pericles*, the similarity with the reign of Henry VIII goes back to Wilkins's original part in the play, in the incestuous relationship between King Antiochus and his unnamed daughter—according to the ugly rumour that may well have reached Shakespeare's ears concerning a similar relationship between Henry and Anne. Even in the plays of the strange intervening period mentioned above, though there is no apparent reference to Henry's England in the "Roman" plays, there is in *Macbeth*, if we may interpret the masterpiece of confusion noted by Macduff in Duncan's murder in terms of the vastly greater sacrilege committed by Henry VIII against all the shrines and monasteries in England. Instead of Henry himself, however, we may find an apparent reflection of his daughter Elizabeth both in the ruthlessness of Lady Macbeth and in the cunning of Cleopatra. Finally, on looking back to the two great tragedies, *Othello* and *King Lear*, at the beginning of the Jacobean age, we may recognize in their two flawed heroes something of Henry VIII, while of the two heroines Desdemona is closer in spirit to Katharine—and in both of them we may see (more abstractly) the Catholic faith of mediaeval England at once represented and rejected.

These are not, however, just ingenious topicalities, discerned in the Jacobean plays out of an academic desire to find allegorical correspondences. Rather, they indicate how deeply the dramatist was affected as a loyal Catholic from his early boyhood both by experience of the intolerable persecution of his fellow-Catholics at the hands of Queen Elizabeth and her "cruel ministers", such as Lord Burghley, and by reflection on the origins of that long drawn out tragedy going back to "the king's great matter" of his divorce from Queen Katharine. Too much ink has been spilt about abstract "reasons" for Shakespeare's greatness as a dramatic genius, without realizing how deeply human genius is rooted in the particularities of one's historical circumstances. Never was a critic more deeply deceived than Ben Jonson, when he pronounced that Shakespeare was "not of an age, but for all time". Nor, by contrast, was another critic more accurate than George Bernard Shaw when he conceived Shakespeare's greatness in terms of his age and nation. Of course, in the continuing situation under King James I, Shakespeare was unable to express his thoughts openly, but at least during the years of persecution under Queen Elizabeth he had grown inured to the art of saying one thing and meaning another, or as George Herbert says in "Jordan", of "catching the sense at two removes". The same art, though subject to the sneers of agnostic scholars in a democratic age and nation, has been cultivated up till recent times in Communist countries such as Poland, when authors had to be continually on their guard (as in Shakespeare's England) against spies and informers.

This must have been a grievous affliction for a poet like Shakespeare, who could express his feelings only in laments such as Hamlet's "But break, my heart, for I must hold my tongue!" Yet he was also aware, with his exiled duke in *As You Like It*, how to find sweetness in "the uses of adversity" and greatness in the need of maintaining an ironic, enigmatic, mysterious persona—for which he had an example in his great Tudor predecessor Sir Thomas More, who reappears in so many of the last plays, till he is actually mentioned by name in *Henry VIII*.

In brief, and in conclusion, it may be said that in all the Jacobean plays, especially the tragedies, the genius of Shakespeare consists in the lending of his poetic voice to what he sees as the sorrowful decline and downfall of Catholic England—that is, of all he most valued from his early boyhood in the historical traditions of his native country—owing to the Machiavellian policies of a few unprincipled individuals, Thomas Cromwell behind Henry VIII, Sir William Cecil behind Queen Elizabeth, and Cecil's son Sir Robert Cecil, who remained behind King James till his death in 1612. Shakespeare's own principle on this point may perhaps best be summarized in the image of a river he puts into the mouth of the heroine Julia in one of his earliest comedies, *The Two Gentlemen of Verona,* "The current that with gentle murmur glides, / Thou know'st, being stopp'd, impatiently doth rage, / But when his fair course is not hindered, / He makes sweet music with th'enamell'd stones, / Giving a gentle kiss to every sedge / He overtaketh in his pilgrimage." (ii.7).

Appendices

appendix 1
Classical Comments on Shakespeare

Ben Jonson (1572–1637)

From his verses prefixed to the First Folio of 1623: "To the memory of my beloved, The Author Mr. William Shakespeare." "The wonder of our stage . . . / Thou art a monument without a tomb, / And art alive still, while thy book doth live . . . / And though thou hadst small Latin and less Greek . . . / He was not of an age but for all time . . . / Yet must I not give Nature all. Thy Art, / My gentle Shakespeare, must bear a part . . . / Sweet Swan of Avon!"

From his *Timber, or Discoveries* (1640): "The players have often mentioned it as an honour to Shakespeare, that in his writing (whatsoever he penned) he never blotted out a line. My answer hath been, Would he had blotted out a thousand. . . . I loved the man, and do honour his memory on this side idolatry, as much as any. He was indeed honest, and of an open and free nature, and had an excellent fantasy, brave notions and gentle expressions, wherein he flowed with that facility that sometimes it was necessary that he should be stopped."

John Milton (1608–74)

From *L'Allegro* (c.1631): "Or sweetest Shakespeare, Fancy's child, / Warble his native woodnotes wild."

From "An Epitaph on the admirable dramatic poet, W. Shakespeare", attached to the Second Folio of 1632. "What needs my Shakespeare for his honour'd bones, / The labour of an age, in piled stones / Or that his hallowed relics should be hid / Under a star ypointing pyramid? . . . / Thou in our wonder and astonishment / Hast built thyself a live-long monument . . . / And so sepulchred in such pomp dost lie / That kings for such a tomb would wish to die."

John Dryden (1631–1700)

From his *Essay of Dramatic Poesy* (1668): "To begin then with Shakespeare, he was the man who of all modern and perhaps ancient poets had the largest and most comprehensive soul. All the images of Nature were still present to him and he drew them not laboriously but luckily. When he describes anything, you more than see it, you feel it too. Those who accuse him to have wanted learning give him the greater commendation. He was naturally learned. He needed not the spectacles of books to read Nature. He looked inwards and found her there."

From the Prologue to *Aureng-Zebe* (1675): "But spite of all his pride, a secret shame / Invades his breast at Shake-speare's sacred name."

Joseph Addison (1672–1719)

From *The Spectator* (July 1712): "Among the English Shake-speare has incomparably excelled all others. That noble extravagance of fancy, which he had in so great perfection, thoroughly qualified him to touch this weak superstitious part of his reader's imagination, and made him capable of succeeding, where he had nothing to support him besides the strength of his own genius. There is something so wild and yet so solemn in the speeches of his ghosts, fairies, witches and the like imaginary persons that we cannot forbear thinking them natural and must confess, if there are such beings in the world, it looks highly probable they should talk and act as he has represented them."

Alexander Pope (1688–1744)

From his Preface to *The Works of Shakespeare* (1725): "If ever any author deserved the name of an original, it was Shakespeare. . . . The poetry of Shakespeare was inspiration indeed. He is not so much an imitator, as an instrument, of Nature. And 'tis not so just to say that he speaks from her, as that she speaks through him. The characters are so much Nature herself that 'tis a sort of injury to call them by so distant a name as copies of her. . . . Every single character in Shakespeare is as much an individual as those in life itself."

From Epistle "To Augustus" (1737): "Shakespeare (whom you and every play-house bill / Style the divine, the matchless, what you will) / For gain, not glory, wing'd his roving flight / And grew immortal in his own despite."

Samuel Johnson (1707–84)

From his *Preface to Shakespeare* (1765): "Shakespeare is above all writers, at least above all modern writers, the poet of Nature, the poet that holds up to his readers a faithful mirror of manners and of life. His characters are not modified by the customs of particular places, unpractised by the rest of the world, by the peculiarities of studies or professions, which can operate but upon small numbers, or by the accidents of transient fashions or temporary opinions. They are the genuine progeny of common humanity, such as the world will always supply and observation will always find.

"Shakespeare's plays are not in the rigorous and critical sense either tragedies or comedies but compositions of a distinct kind, exhibiting the real state of sublunary Nature, which partakes of good and evil, joy and sorrow, mingled with endless variety and innumerable modes of combination and expressing the course of the world, in which the loss of one is the gain of another. . . . Shakespeare has united the powers of exciting laughter and sorrow not only in one mind but in one composition. Almost all his plays are divided between serious and ludicrous characters, and in the successive evolution of the design sometimes produce seriousness and sorrow, and sometimes levity and laughter."

"His first defect is that to which may be imputed most of the evil in books or in men. He sacrifices virtue to convenience, and is so much more careful to please than to instruct, that he seems to write without any moral purpose. From his writings indeed a system of moral duty may be selected, for he that thinks reasonably must think morally. But his precepts and axioms drop casually from him, he makes no just distribution of good or evil, nor is always careful to show in the virtuous a disapprobation of the wicked. He carries his persons indifferently through right and wrong, and at the close dismisses them without further care and leaves their examples to operate by chance."

"A quibble is to Shakespeare what luminous vapours are to the traveler. He follows it at all adventures. It is sure to lead him out of his way and sure to engulf him in the mire. It has some malignant power over his mind, and its fascinations are irresistible. Whatever be the dignity or profundity of his disquisition, whether he be enlarging knowledge or exalting affection, whether he be amusing attention with incidents or enchaining it in suspense, let but a quibble spring up before him, and he leaves his work unfinished. A quibble is the golden apple for which he will always turn aside from his career or stoop from his elevation. A quibble, poor and barren as it is, gave him such delight that he was content to purchase it by the sacrifice of reason, propriety and truth. A quibble was to him the fatal Cleopatra for which he lost the world, and was content to lose it."

William Wordsworth (1770–1850)

From *Miscellaneous Sonnets* Part I. xxx: "It is a beauteous evening" (1807). "We must be free or die, who speak the tongue / That Shakespeare spake, the faith and morals hold / Which Milton held."

Ibid. Part I, i. (1827): "Scorn not the sonnet. Critic, you have frowned, / Mindless of its just honours. With this key / Shakespeare unlocked his heart." (But cf. R. Browning, *House* [1876]. " 'With this same key / Shakespeare unlocked his heart' once more! / Did Shakespeare? If so, the less Shakespeare he!")

Samuel Taylor Coleridge (1772–1834)

From *Biographia Literaria* (1817): "Shakespeare, no mere child of Nature, no automaton of genius, no passive vehicle of inspiration possessed by the spirit, not possessing it, first studied patiently, meditated deeply, understood minutely, till knowledge, become habitual and intuitive, wedded itself to his habitual feelings and at length gave birth to that stupendous power by which he stands alone, with no equal or second in his own class."

Ibid.: "Our myriad-minded Shakespeare. . . . No man was ever yet a great poet, without being at the same time a profound philosopher."

From *Lectures* (publ. 1883): "I am deeply convinced that no man, however wide his erudition, however patient his antiquarian researches, can possibly understand, or be worthy of understanding, the writings of Shakespeare."

From *Table-Talk* (March 1834): "I believe Shakespeare was not a whit more intelligible in his own day that he is now to an educated man, except for a few local allusions of no consequence. He is of no age—nor of any religion, or party, or profession. The body and substance of his works came out of the unfathomable depths of his own oceanic mind. His observation and reading, which was considerable, supplied him with the drapery of his figures."

Thomas de Quincey (1785–1859)

From his essay "On the Knocking at the Gate in *Macbeth*" (1823): "From my boyish days I had always felt a great perplexity on one point in *Macbeth*. It was this. The knocking at the gate, which succeeds the murder of Duncan produced to my feelings an effect for which I could never account. The effect was that it reflected back upon the murderer a peculiar awfulness and a depth of solemnity. Yet however obstinately I endeavoured with my understanding to comprehend this, for many years I could never see why it should produce such an effect."

John Keats (1795–1821)

From his *Letters* (1817–20): "It struck me what quality went to form a man of achievement, especially in literature, and which Shakespeare possessed so enormously. I mean negative capability, that is, when a man is capable of being in uncertainties, mysteries and doubts, without any irritable reaching after fact and reason."

Ibid.: "Shakespeare led a life of allegory. His works are the comment on it."

Thomas Carlyle (1795–1881)

From his lectures on *Heroes and Hero-Worship*, III, "The Hero as Poet" (1840): "Whoever looks intelligently at this Shakespeare may recognize that he too was a prophet, in his way, of an insight analogous to the prophetic, though he took it up in another strain. Nature seemed to this man also divine, unspeakable, deep as Tophet, high as Heaven. . . . We called Dante the melodious priest of Middle-Age Catholicism. May we not call Shakespeare the still more melodious priest of a true Catholicism, the Universal Church of the future and of all times?"

Ibid.: "Indian Empire, or no Indian Empire, we cannot do without Shakespeare. Indian Empire will go, at any rate, some day. But this Shakespeare does not go, he lasts forever with us. We cannot give up our Shakespeare! . . . Yes, this Shakespeare is ours, we produced him, we speak and think by him, we are of one blood and kind with him."

John Henry Newman (1801–90)

From *The Idea of a University* (1873): "There surely is in all of us a cause for thankfulness that the most illustrious amongst English writers has so little of a Protestant about him that Catholics have been able without extravagance to claim him as their own, and that enemies to our creed have allowed that he is only not a Catholic because, and as far as, his times forbade it. . . . There is in Shakespeare neither contempt of religion nor skepticism, and he upholds the broad laws of moral and divine truth."

Matthew Arnold (1822–88)

From sonnet "Shakespeare" (1849): "Others abide our question. Thou art free. / We ask and ask—thou smilest and art still, / Out-topping knowledge."

Gerard Manley Hopkins (1844–89)

From *Letters* to Baillie (1864): "Shakespeare is and must be utterly the greatest of poets." To Dixon (1881). "After all it is the breadth of his human nature that we admire in Shakespeare." To Dixon (1883): "I think Shakespeare's drama is more in this sense romantic than the Greek, and that if unity of action is not so marked (as it is not) the interest of *romance*, arising from a well-calculated strain of incidents, is greater."

George Bernard Shaw (1856–1950)

From *Dramatic Opinions* (1907): "With the single exception of Homer, there is no eminent writer, not even Sir Walter Scott, whom I can despise so entirely as I despise Shakespeare when I measure my mind against his. . . . It would positively be a relief to me to dig him up and throw stones at him."

From *The Sanity of Art* (1908): "The writer who aims at producing the platitudes which are 'not for an age but for all time' has his reward in being unreadable in all ages, whilst Plato and Aristophanes trying to knock some sense into the Athens of their day, Shakespeare peopling that same Athens with Elizabethan mechanics and Warwickshire hunts . . . are still alive and at home everywhere among the dust and ashes of many thousands of academic, punctilious, most archaeologically correct men of letters and art who spent their lives haughtily avoiding the journalist's vulgar obsession with the ephemeral."

Gilbert Keith Chesterton (1874–1936)

From *Chaucer* (1932): "That Shakespeare was a Catholic is a thing that every Catholic feels by every sort of convergent common sense to be true. It is supported by the few external and political facts we know, it is utterly unmistakable in the general spirit and atmosphere."

Ibid.: "The Renaissance genius was never so much intellectually inspired as when he seemed to be intellectually intoxicated, and his very depression was an exaltation. It would be something to be able even to despair like one of Shakespeare's characters. A dying man might want to live, if he could go on producing such phrases as 'Absent thee from felicity awhile'. He might even continue to absent himself. A murderer might grow cheerful, if he were able to utter his misery in those words about life being a thing 'full of sound and fury, signifying nothing'."

From *A Handful of Authors* (1953), "The Heroines of Shakespeare": "In this one virtue (of purity), in this one sex (of woman), something heroic and holy, something in the highest sense of the word fabulous, was felt to reside. Man was natural, but woman was supernatural."

Thomas Stearns Eliot (1888–1965)

From his essay on "Hamlet" (1919): "So far from being Shakespeare's masterpiece, the play is most certainly an artistic failure. . . . *Coriolanus* may not be as 'interesting' as *Hamlet*, but it is, with *Antony and Cleopatra*, Shakespeare's most assured artistic success. And probably more people have thought *Hamlet* a work of art because they found it interesting, than have found it interesting because it is a work of art. It is the 'Mona Lisa' of literature."

Ibid.: "The only way of expressing emotion in the form of art is by finding an 'objective correlative'—in other words, a set of objects, a situation, a chain of events which shall be the formula of that *particular* emotion, such that when the external facts, which must terminate in sensory experience, are given, the emotion is immediately evoked."

From his essay on "Dante" (1929): "There is an opacity, or inspissation of poetic style throughout Europe after the Renaissance."

Ibid.: "We do not understand Shakespeare from a single reading, and certainly not from a single play. There is a relation between the various plays of Shakespeare, taken in order. And it is a work of years to venture even one individual interpretation of the pattern in Shakespeare's carpet. . . . It is not certain that Shakespeare himself knew what it was."

Graham Greene (1904–91)

From Introduction to *The Autobiography of a Hunted Priest*, by John Gerard (1952): "Isn't there one whole area of the Elizabethan scene that we miss in Shakespeare's huge world of comedy and despair? The kings speak, the adventurers speak . . . the madmen and the lovers, the soldiers and the poets, but the martyrs are quite silent."

appendix 2
A Bibliography on Shakespeare and Christianity

Books Based on Groupings of Shakespeare's Plays

THE "FOUR GREAT TRAGEDIES" were famously dealt with as a group by A. C. Bradley in his authoritative *Shakespearean Tragedy* (1904), but already the four "Problem Plays" had been discussed by F. R. Boas in his *Shakespeare and His Predecessors* (1896). Later on, E. M. W. Tillyard published three such books: *Shakespeare's History Plays* (1944), with the division of his material into two main tetralogies covering the history of England from the reign of Richard II to that of Richard III; *Shakespeare's Problem Plays* (1971), following the same selection as that made by Boas; and *Shakespeare's Last Plays* (1938), dealing chiefly with *Cymbeline, The Winter's Tale,* and *The Tempest*. A better grouping for the last plays, which should at least include *Pericles*, is that proposed by R. G. Hunter in his *Shakespeare and the Comedy of Forgiveness* (1965). Here, to my shame, I have to confess I have followed most of these groupings in my first book on Shakespeare, *An Introduction to Shakespeare's Plays* (1964).

Christian Interpretations of Shakespeare's Plays

Among the many such books that came out after World War II, I may begin with George Wilson Knight's *The Crown of Life* (1947) on the final plays, then John Danby's *Shakespeare's Doctrine of Nature* (1949) especially in *King Lear*, M. D. Parker's fine study of *The Slave of Life* (1955), Paul Siegel's *Shakespearean Tragedy and the Elizabethan Compromise* (1957), John Vyvyan's *The Shakespearian Ethic* (1959), Maynard Mack's *King Lear in Our Time* (1965), and notably Roy Battenhouse's *Shakespearean Tragedy, Its Art and Its Christian Premises* (1969)—followed by his later anthology of *Shakespeare's Christian Dimension* (1993), including a contribution of mine on *King Lear*.

This approach, however, suffered an ironical setback with the publication of Roland Frye's *Shakespeare and Christian Doctrine* (1963), justifying a purely secular approach from the viewpoint of three major Reformation theologians, Luther, Calvin, and Hooker, and specifically attacking what he termed "the School of Knight". His book was shortly followed by W. R. Elton's *King Lear and the Gods* (1965), proposing an agnostic approach to this dramatic masterpiece, with abundant documentation from contemporary writings. From then onwards this approach became the "orthodoxy" of the Shakespeare "establishment", now beginning to organize itself worldwide, and coming to a climax in Samuel Schoenbaum's *Shakespeare, A Documentary Life* (1975).

Shakespeare and the Bible

Meanwhile, for books on Shakespeare's use of the Bible, we have to go back to the Victorian Bishop Charles Wordsworth (the poet's nephew) with his *Shakespeare's Knowledge and Use of the Bible* (1864), to Thomas Carter's *Shakespeare and Holy Scripture* (1905), and to the more authoritative Richmond

Noble's *Shakespeare's Biblical Knowledge* (1935). Partly relying on these three books, I published my own study of *Biblical Themes in Shakespeare* (1975), before going on to make a more special study of *Biblical Influence in the Great Tragedies* (1985), which was republished in America in 1986 under the altered title of *Biblical Influences in Shakespeare's Great Tragedies*. At the same time, Naseeb Shaheen in America brought out his *Biblical References in Shakespeare's Tragedies* (1987), following it up with other books on *Shakespeare's History Plays* (1989) and *Shakespeare's Comedies* (1993). Of all these books I may claim that mine alone brings out the impact of biblical influence on the thematic meaning of the plays.

Shakespeare and Catholicism

The special study of Shakespeare's Catholic allegiance goes back to the Victorian scholar-friend of Newman, Richard Simpson, whose notes on the subject were used by a priest of the Oratory, Henry Bowden, in his book on *The Religion of Shakespeare* (1899). A more general survey of the poet's religious formation was undertaken by John Henry de Groot, a Protestant minister, in *The Shakespeares and 'The Old Faith'* (1946), and a more thorough study of the poet's religion in relation to his friends and acquaintances, by two German scholars, Heinrich Mutschmann and Karl Wentersdorf, translated into English as *Shakespeare and Catholicism* (1952). Here I came into the field with my wider study of *Shakespeare's Religious Background* (1973), considering the extent to which the various religious influences of his age, Catholic, Protestant, Puritan, and even "atheistic", have entered into the plays, while concluding that on balance the Catholic element is the strongest. This book I subsequently followed up with two bibliographical studies of *The Religious*

Controversies of the Elizabethan Age (1977) and *Religious Controversies of the Jacobean Age* (1978). My interpretation was subsequently supported by Ian Wilson in his biographical survey of *Shakespeare, the Evidences* (1993), the only biography of Shakespeare written from a Catholic viewpoint. I then came out more into the open with two books proposing a Catholic interpretation of the plays, *The Catholicism of Shakespeare's Plays* (1997) and *Shakespeare's Apocalypse* (2000) on the four tragedies. In the same year Carol Enos, though not herself a Catholic, published her book on *Shakespeare and the Catholic Religion*. More recently I have devoted two books to the related subject of "meta-drama", as seen in detail in Shakespeare's great tragedies, *Shakespeare's Meta-drama—Hamlet and Macbeth* (2003) and *Shakespeare's Meta-drama—Othello and King Lear* (2004). Then there is my latest book on *Shakespeare the Papist* (2005), which came out simultaneously and coincidentally with Clare Asquith's *Shadowplay*.

Shakespeare's Catholic Formation and the Shakeshafte Theory

Over the past few decades a certain theory has come to the fore applying the old tradition, that the young Shakespeare had been "a schoolmaster in the country", to a certain gifted young tutor-player whose name had been found mentioned in a will, dated 1581, of a Catholic gentleman in Lancashire, Alexander Houghton of Lea Hall near Preston. It was seemingly refuted by the criticism of Schoenbaum in his authoritative biography but subsequently revived by E. A. J. Honigmann with answering scholarship in his meticulous study of *Shakespeare, The 'Lost Years'* (1986)—incidentally supporting my arguments in favour of the theory against Schoenbaum's rebuttal of them. His work paved the way for an important conference held at the University of Lancaster in 1999 on

"Lancastrian Shakespeare", which practically meant "Shakespeare's Catholic Background", since only a reliable Catholic would have been trusted as tutor and player in such a Catholic household. The proceedings of this conference have at last been published under the title of *Lancastrian Shakespeare* (2003) in two volumes, including a paper of mine on "Shakespeare's Jesuit Schoolmasters"—considering how many of the masters at the Stratford Grammar School were connected both with the Jesuits and with Lancashire. Interestingly, the following year another conference on "Shakespeare and Religions" was held at Stratford, and the proceedings published in the subsequent issue of *The Shakespeare Survey* (2001)—including another contribution of mine on "Religion in Arden". Yet another contribution of mine, based on the probable meeting of Shakespeare and Campion in Lancashire, came out as a monograph entitled *The Plays and the Exercises—A Hidden Source of Shakespeare's Inspiration?* (2002). Subsequently, there appeared an anthology of essays by American scholars on the same subject under the title *Shakespeare and the Culture of Christianity in Early Modern England* (2003), which was dedicated to me as a pioneer in this field. Today it is still a very live subject, all the more as it has for so long been suppressed under a kind of taboo by "orthodox" scholars, as belonging to the "lunatic fringe" of Shakespeare studies.

Subject Index

See also *Index of Characters* for references
to *dramatis personae* in plays

Character Index

See also *Subject Index*, for characters who are also real persons